TERRY SHEPHERD'S PODCAST ESSENTIALS

TERRY SHEPHERD

This is dedicated to all the aspiring podcasters out there, the dreamers, the creators, the ones who dare to share their voices with the world. To those who tirelessly work behind the scenes, mastering the art of audio engineering, honing their interviewing skills, and refining their storytelling abilities. This is for the individuals who understand that podcasting is more than just a hobby; it's a passion, a calling, a way to connect with others and leave a lasting impact. It's for the individuals who are brave enough to put themselves out there, to share their perspectives, and to build a community around their shared interests. This book is a testament to your dedication, your perseverance, and your unwavering belief in the power of audio storytelling. It is a guide to help navigate the exciting and sometimes challenging world of podcast creation and distribution, empowering you to create a podcast that truly resonates with your listeners and achieves your goals. This is for you – the future voices of the podcasting world. May this book serve as your companion and resource on your journey.

Terry Shepherd - Jacksonville, FL - March 2025

INTRODUCTION

First things first. This book is *not* about video podcasts. I've created them. I've analyzed their effectiveness. I don't believe that long-form video interviews hold an audience in our short-attention span world.

My own experience in the video space taught me that while I could generate a lot of "views," the amount of time spent actually watching the shows often totaled less than thirty seconds. When you consider that video podcasts *done right* take hours to record, edit and produce, the return on time and effort often isn't worth it.

Reels and Shorts are a different animal. These brief 30 to 90 second video selections highlighting an important point or selling the story in a short burst can be highly successful. If your recording platform allows for both video and audio, consider asking guests for permission to lift a "magic moment" for use in a Reel, then use that to promote your audio-only product.

Should you go it alone?

This book's goal is to take you inside every aspect of creating, recording and distributing content. It assumes you'll do it all yourself.

But should you?

There are a growing number of professional producers who have created rate cards to fit every budget. Producers can assist with scheduling, managing the recording platform, editing and even creating the metadata and uploading your program for distribution.

The old-saying that we should "outsource our weaknesses" has value here, especially if podcasting is just one of many things on your plate. As with every other recommendation in this book, I encourage you to throughly research the contributions and costs associated with hiring outside help.

Finding and managing other people requires your time and energy. But if you have the budget, anything you can avoid that keeps you from your most important role, the host, could possibly be done by others.

What is it about audio that is so appealing?

Podcasts have transcended their niche origins to become a mainstream medium, captivating millions with their intimate and engaging format. They offer a connection between creator and listener, fostering a sense of community and shared experience unlike any other form of media.

That said, creating a successful podcast requires more than just a good idea and a microphone. You'll need a strategic approach, meticulous planning, and a deep understanding of your audience. This book is a comprehensive guide to mastering the art and science of podcasting. We'll delve into every aspect of podcast production, from initial brainstorming and concept development to the final stages of distribution and promotion. We'll cover the technical essentials—selecting the right equipment, mastering audio editing software, and choosing a suitable hosting platform—while also exploring the creative aspects—developing compelling content, mastering interviewing techniques, and building a loyal audience. We'll explore the process of defining your niche, identifying your target audience, and creating a compelling brand identity that sets your podcast apart from the competition. This isn't just about learning the mechanics; it's about understanding the strategy, the storytelling, and the community-building elements that will propel your podcast to success. Throughout the book, you'll find practical exercises, real-world examples, and actionable advice gleaned from years of experience in the industry. So, whether you're a complete beginner or an experienced podcaster looking to elevate your game, prepare to embark on a transformative journey into the world of audio storytelling. Let's begin crafting the podcast of your dreams.

PART I

PART 1 - DEFINING YOUR PODCAST AND UNDERSTANDING YOUR AUDIENCE

1
IDENTIFYING YOUR PODCAST NICHE AND PURPOSE

Before you dive into buying microphones, audio interfaces, and editing software, let's take some time to clearly define the niche and purpose for your podcast. If you were building a house, you wouldn't start constructing walls before laying a proper foundation. The same holds true for your podcast. Without that foundation, it's likely to crumble under the weight of production challenges and a lack of audience engagement.

BRAINSTORMING NICHE AND PURPOSE

Do yourself a favor, and take time for some introspection. Get out a pen and paper and start brainstorming. What are you truly passionate about? What knowledge or skills do you possess that others might find valuable or entertaining? Who else is podcasting about it? What would make your show distinctive?

Don't underestimate the power of your special perspective. Your personal experiences, hobbies, and professional expertise are all potential springboards for a compelling podcast. Brainstorm freely, jotting down every idea that comes to mind, no matter how outlandish it might seem initially.

MARKET RESEARCH AND VIABILITY

Once you have a list of potential topics, it's time to evaluate their viability. This involves engaging in the all-important process of market research. Are other podcasts already covering similar ground? If so, what makes your approach different? What noteworthy angle can you bring to the table? A successful podcast needs a unique selling proposition (USP) to set it apart from the competition. This USP is your podcast's promise to the listener; it's the reason they'll choose your show over others.

Let's consider some examples. Suppose you're passionate about vintage motorcycles. A podcast titled "Vintage Motorcycles" is too broad. Instead, you might consider a niche, something like: "Restoring Classic British Bikes," "The History of Harley-Davidson," or "Motorcycle Maintenance for Beginners." Each of these titles focuses on a specific target audience, and attracting listeners who will love what you have to share.

As another example, suppose your expertise lies in organic gardening. "Organic Gardening" would be too broad, so instead you might focus on "Vertical Gardening in Small Spaces," "Organic Pest Control Methods," or "Growing Heirloom Tomatoes." The more specific your niche, the easier it is to target your marketing efforts and attract a loyal following.

Analyze competitor podcasts. Search out and listen to several podcasts in your chosen niche. What works well? What could be improved? What gaps exist in the market that your podcast could fill? Look at their audience engagement strategies. How do they interact with listeners? Do they solicit feedback? Do they run contests or give-aways? Learn from their successes and avoid their mistakes.

You don't want to try to copy an existing podcast; you do want to understand the dynamics of your chosen niche and craft a strategy that will allow your podcast to thrive.

VALIDATING YOUR CONCEPT

A successful podcast isn't just about your passion; it's about aligning that passion with a market need. Now that you've identified your potential niche and honed your USP, it's time to validate your concept and make sure there is a market for it. Creating a simple survey or conducting brief interviews with potential listeners can be incredibly valuable. Ask them if they would be interested in a podcast covering your chosen topic. Seek feedback on potential episode ideas and formats.

I urge you not to skip this step. Your research will confirm (or not!) your assumptions about the market demand for your podcast. If you receive negative feedback or there's a lack of interest, don't be discouraged. This is great information! You can use it to refine your concept and make it even stronger.

Consider a podcast about the history of obscure board games. While this is a niche topic, is there enough audience interest to support a podcast? Market research will tell you the answer. Perhaps you discover that the audience is there but concentrated within specific online forums or social media groups. This intel will help you create a successful marketing strategy, with your efforts directed towards those specific communities.

Another question to consider is how you will maintain consistency and freshness within your niche. A podcast about a narrow topic like "The History of Antique Typewriters" will require some creative thinking to avoid running out of steam. Will you focus on specific models? Interview collectors? Explore the social history around typewriters? Developing a detailed content strategy early on will help ensure that your podcast remains engaging for both you and your listeners over the long haul.

THE TAKE-AWAY

This initial planning phase is not simply a checklist to complete; it's a living document that should be revised and refined as your podcast evolves. Be open to adjusting your focus as you learn more about your audience and the podcasting landscape. Regularly analyze your listener feedback and adjust your strategy accordingly. Flexibility is key to sustainability. This dynamic approach ensures that your podcast remains relevant, engaging, and successful. Your passion is the fuel, but your market research is the compass guiding you to your destination.

2

UNDERSTANDING YOUR IDEAL LISTENER

WHO IS YOUR P1?

In the radio business the term P1 is used to describe the ideal listener. As a Top-40 announcer, I was profoundly interested in researching who were my most dedicated listeners and how I could connect with them. Back then, we had one resource we depended on: the rating book, which told us what demographic segments listened and when they listened.

I wanted more information, so I made a point of circulating in places where I knew (or imagined) my P1s might be. I participated in record hops (which were popular then), emceed events, and attended activities and concerts where I thought my listeners might be. I engaged with them to help me understand what they liked—and equally importantly, what they didn't like—and why.

As a podcaster, it's equally important to understand your ideal listener, and guessing is not going to cut it. You need a detailed picture, a persona or avatar for your listener that guides every aspect of your podcast's creation and marketing. This involves going beyond simple demographics and delving into the values, interests, and lifestyles of your target audience. Ideally, you're going to create a detailed profile of a listener so real that you can easily imagine them sitting down to listen to your podcast.

The first step is to define your target audience using demographic factors. Who are you trying to reach? Consider age ranges, geographic locations, and income levels. Are you targeting young professionals in urban areas? Retired individuals in rural communities? Mothers of young children? The more specific you are, the better you can tailor your content and marketing efforts.

For example, a podcast about financial planning for millennials will have a vastly different approach than one geared towards retirees. Consider the technological proficiency of your target audience. Are they comfortable with various podcast apps and platforms, or will you need to simplify your delivery methods?

Demographics alone won't provide a complete picture, so let's move onto a process often used in marketing: psychographics. Psychographics involves using psychology to study people's attitudes, interests, and behaviors. What motivates them? What are their concerns? What kind of information are they seeking? Consider their media consumption habits. Do they prefer short-form or long-form content? What other podcasts do they listen to? Are they active on social media? Understanding their psychographic profile allows you to tailor your content to their specific needs and interests, enhancing engagement and resonance.

For instance, a podcast about sustainable living could target environmentally conscious individuals, particularly those interested in reducing their carbon footprint. This goes beyond simply stating the age or income of your listener; it delves into their motivations—their desire for a healthier planet and a sustainable lifestyle. Similarly, a podcast focusing on personal finance might target individuals striving for financial independence, highlighting the value of saving and investing. Understanding these underlying motivations allows you to connect with your listeners on a deeper, more meaningful level.

Let's examine several examples of creating listener personas. Consider a podcast about historical fiction:

Persona 1: The Avid Reader: This listener is probably older, well-educated, and enjoys immersing themselves in historical narratives. They appreciate in-depth discussions of historical context and are interested in learning more about the historical periods depicted in the books. They value accuracy and enjoy podcasts that bring historical novels to life. Their preferred format is likely a longer, more detailed analysis of a specific book. Their social media presence might lean towards book clubs and historical fiction fan groups.

Persona 2: The Casual Listener: This listener may be younger, less invested in historical accuracy, and more interested in the storytelling aspect. They appreciate shorter, more easily digestible discussions and may prefer podcasts that focus on broader themes like romance, adventure, or mystery. They might follow podcasts for entertainment during their commute or while doing chores. Their social media presence might be more casual, possibly with fewer ties to specific book groups.

Let's try something different now—a podcast about classic rock

Persona 1: The Vinyl Veteran: This listener is likely older, has a vast record collection, and is looking for deep dives into obscure bands, lost albums, and the technical aspects of recording and production. They value in-depth discussions, possibly involving historical context. They may seek podcasts that explore niche subgenres within classic rock or focus on specific geographic scenes. They may enjoy a podcast that challenges established opinions on classic rock artists. Their social media presence might involve engagement with other collectors, participation in online forums dedicated to specific bands, and sharing rare finds.

Persona 2: The Casual Rocker: This listener is likely younger, with a more general appreciation for classic rock's biggest hits. They prefer easily digestible content focusing on iconic artists and memorable songs. They may be interested in podcasts covering the "greatest hits" of various bands or exploring the stories behind famous albums. Their social media presence might involve sharing their favorite songs, participating in polls about classic rock artists, and engaging with lighter, more general classic rock content.

Creating personas like these allows you to tailor your content specifically to your audience. For example, the "Vinyl Veteran" might appreciate a segment dedicated to analyzing the mastering techniques used on a specific album, whereas the "Casual Rocker" might prefer a focus on the band's most popular songs and their cultural impact. Similarly, the "Vinyl Veteran" might appreciate a discussion on the influence of a particular producer on a specific subgenre, while the "Casual Rocker" would benefit from a simple overview of a band's career highlights.

So how do you uncover this very important information? By using a variety of research techniques. I've listed some valuable information gathering techniques below, but you may well be able to think of others. Put on your creative thinking hat and dive in!

Surveys: Use online survey tools to gather quantitative data about your target audience. Ask questions about their age, location, income, interests, and podcast listening habits.

Social Media Polls: Engage your audience on platforms like Twitter, Instagram, or Facebook with polls and interactive quizzes to gain insights into their preferences and needs.

Analyze Listener Data: If you're already producing a podcast, leverage analytics data from your hosting platform to understand listener demographics, engagement metrics, and episode performance.

Focus Groups: Organize small group discussions with potential listeners to gather qualitative data about their thoughts, opinions, and suggestions.

One-on-one Interviews: Conduct in-depth interviews with

a select group of potential listeners to gain deeper insights into their motivations and needs.

However you go about gathering your information, be sure to gather both quantitative data (numbers and statistics) and qualitative data (opinions and insights) to paint a complete picture of your listener. These data points, when analyzed systematically, allow you to fine-tune your podcast content and improve its resonance with your audience.

Once you've created detailed listener personas, the next step is to actively incorporate them into your podcast strategy. This means consciously tailoring the content, format, tone, and even the marketing materials to appeal to your defined ideal listeners. For example, if you've identified a significant portion of your audience as busy professionals, you might produce shorter, more concise episodes that fit into their hectic schedules. If you've discovered that your audience values authenticity, make sure your podcast reflects this value through honest and genuine discussions.

Remember to regularly analyze listener feedback. Encourage listener interaction through comments, reviews, and social media engagement. Actively solicit feedback on your podcast's content, format, and overall experience. Use this feedback to refine your listener personas and adjust your podcast strategy accordingly. Remember, your ideal listener isn't static; but is rather a constantly evolving entity that needs continuous refinement. By consistently analyzing data and actively engaging with your listeners, you'll ensure your podcast continues to resonate and succeed.

THE TAKE-AWAY

Don't underestimate the power of data analytics. Most podcast hosting platforms provide data on download numbers, listenership patterns, and even listener demographics. Track this data meticulously, looking for trends and patterns. Which episodes are the most popular? What topics resonate most with your listeners? Which segments are most frequently skipped? This data helps you identify what works and what doesn't, so you can fine-tune your podcast accordingly. It's not just about the numbers; it's about using the numbers to tell a story about your audience's engagement and preferences. This data-driven approach ensures that you remain focused on producing high-quality content that consistently engages your target audience. The process of understanding your ideal listener is ongoing and dynamic; it's a journey, not a destination.

3
WHAT DO I CALL THIS THING?

WHAT'S IN A NAME? CHOOSING YOUR TITLE.

Building on the detailed understanding of your target audience, the next step in launching your podcast is crafting a compelling title and description. These two elements are the first impression your potential listeners will have of your show, the gateway to attracting and retaining an audience. A poorly chosen title or a weak description can significantly hinder your podcast's success, even if the content itself is excellent. Conversely, a well-crafted title and description can dramatically increase your podcast's discoverability and attract the right listeners.

Let's begin with the podcast title. Your title is the single most important piece of branding for your show. It needs to be memorable, concise, and accurately represent the content. Aim for something short, catchy, and easily understood, rather than a long title that is difficult to remember or search for. Consider using keywords that are relevant to your podcast's topic. This will improve your podcast's visibility in search results on podcast platforms like Apple Podcasts, Spotify, and Google Podcasts.

People often search for podcasts using specific keywords, so strategically including these words in your title can significantly increase your podcast's discoverability. There are many internet sites to help you do keyword research. Google Keyword Planner or Ahrefs will get you started.

One popular approach is using a descriptive title, clearly outlining your podcast's topic. For example, "The History of Rock and Roll" or "The Sustainable Gardening Podcast" immediately make it clear what the podcast is about. Another approach is using a more creative or evocative title that captures the essence of your podcast without explicitly stating its subject matter. A good example is "Hidden Histories," which hints at the podcast's focus on historical narratives but allows for a degree of intrigue and mystery. You can also combine descriptive and creative elements to create a title that is both informative and engaging.

Consider your podcast's overall tone and style. A serious, academic podcast might benefit from a formal and descriptive title, while a lighthearted, humorous podcast might be better served by a more playful and creative title. Test out different options, reading them aloud to see how they sound and feel. Get feedback from others; ask friends, colleagues, or potential listeners for their opinions. Their feedback can provide valuable insights into which titles resonate most effectively.

CRAFTING YOUR SHOW DESCRIPTION

After selecting your title, the next critical element is the podcast description. This is your opportunity to entice potential listeners to subscribe to your podcast. You'll need to craft a description that is both informative and engaging. It should succinctly describe what your podcast is about, highlighting its unique value proposition and what listeners can expect. Think of it as the elevator pitch for your podcast. Make sure to share the core value proposition within the first few sentences to capture attention before your potential listener scrolls down or moves on.

Keep your language clear, concise, and easily understood. Avoid using jargon or overly technical language unless it's directly relevant to your target audience. Highlight the key benefits of listening to your podcast. What will listeners learn? How will it benefit them? Will it help them solve a problem? Provide a sense of the podcast's personality and tone. Is it serious and informative, humorous and entertaining, or something else? Incorporate keywords relevant to your podcast's subject matter to improve search engine optimization. Here you'll be looking for a broader range of keywords than you used in your title, terms that are related to specific episodes and their content.

Insert a strong call to action at the end of your description. Encourage potential listeners to subscribe, leave a review, and share your podcast with others. You might include phrases like, "Subscribe now to get the latest episodes delivered straight to your inbox," or "Join the conversation and leave a review to share your thoughts!" Make the call to action clear, concise, and easy to follow. Link to your social media pages if applicable, allowing listeners to engage with you and other members of your podcast community.

Let's look at some examples. Suppose you're launching a podcast about personal finance for young professionals. You've chosen a descriptive title that is straightforward and informative, maybe something like "Millennial Money Matters."

Your description might read:

Navigating the complexities of personal finance can feel overwhelming, especially when you're starting out. Millennial Money Matters simplifies financial planning for young professionals, providing practical tips, advice, and insights to help you achieve your financial goals. From budgeting and saving to investing and debt management, we cover it all. Join us each week for insightful discussions and actionable strategies to improve your financial well-being. Subscribe now and start your journey towards financial freedom!

This description clearly explains the podcast's purpose, target audience, and the value it offers.

Now, let's consider a podcast on historical fiction. A creative title like "Chronicles of Yesterday" might capture more intrigue. The description could read:

Step back in time and immerse yourself in the captivating worlds of historical fiction. Chronicles of Yesterday explores the rich narratives, compelling characters, and historical contexts of some of the most popular historical novels. Join us each week as we delve into the details, discuss plot twists, and uncover the creative liberties and historical realities woven into these stories. Whether you're an avid reader or just beginning your journey into historical fiction, Chronicles of Yesterday offers a special perspective and insightful commentary on the genre.

Subscribe and embark on a captivating journey through the past!

This description emphasizes the podcast's tone and target audience, enticing potential listeners with a sense of adventure and discovery.

The Take-Away

Your title and description are more than just words; they are the face of your podcast. They represent your brand and should reflect the quality and value of your content. Invest the time and effort to craft a compelling title and description that accurately represents your podcast and attracts your target audience. Constantly review and refine your title and description based on listener feedback and analytics to optimize its performance. By consistently analyzing these key elements and adjusting based on data, you'll be well on your way to building a successful and engaging podcast. The continuous refinement of your podcast's branding, just like your understanding of your ideal listener, will contribute to long-term growth and success .

4
CONTENT IS KING!

BRAINSTORMING CONTENT

Building upon the foundation of a compelling title and description, the next step in establishing a thriving podcast is developing a robust content strategy and meticulous episode planning. This phase goes beyond simply having great ideas; it's about a structured, consistent approach to content creation that keeps your audience engaged and coming back for more. A well-defined content strategy is the roadmap to your podcast's success, ensuring that each episode contributes to the overall narrative and reinforces your brand identity.

It's brainstorming time again. Be wide open to all ideas and don't limit yourself at this point; the goal is to generate a broad range of potential topics aligned with your podcast's core theme and your audience's interests. Consider making use of mind mapping techniques or collaborative brainstorming sessions to unlock creative avenues and explore unanticipated angles. Think about current events, topics that are trending within your niche, and frequently asked questions from your audience (if you've already built a small community). Keep a running document, digitally or physically (or both) where you can jot down every idea, regardless of how developed it seems at first. This bank of ideas will be your resource as you refine your content calendar.

Once you have a substantial list of potential episode topics, the next step is to organize and prioritize them. Evaluate each idea based on its relevance to your target audience, its potential impact, and its feasibility. Consider factors such as the availability of resources, the required research time, and the potential for guest collaborations. Categorize your ideas based on themes or subtopics, making it easier to group related episodes and create a sense of progression throughout your podcast's narrative. This organization will create a cohesive and engaging listening experience.

EPISODE FORMAT

Defining your episode formats is another important aspect of content strategy. Will your episodes primarily feature solo presentations, interviews with experts, panel discussions, or a mix of different formats? Each format has its own strengths and weaknesses, and the best approach will depend on your content and your overall podcast goals.

Solo shows offer a great degree of control and allow you to deliver your message directly to your audience without interruption. They are ideal for sharing personal anecdotes, offering expert opinions, or teaching specific skills. However, the lack of diverse perspectives might limit listener engagement for some audiences.

Interviews with experts or influential figures in your field can add credibility and variety to your podcast. Guest interviews provide perspectives and can attract a wider audience through cross-promotion. Careful planning is necessary to ensure a smooth and engaging conversation, including pre-interview preparation and well-defined questions. Remember to always secure permission for recording and usage of the interview.

Panel discussions, involving multiple guests with diverse viewpoints, can create dynamic and engaging conversations. They offer a rich tapestry of perspectives and can spark lively debate, making for a more compelling listen. However, managing multiple participants requires skillful moderation and careful planning to maintain focus and structure.

Regardless of the format, it's important to maintain a consistent release schedule.

Regular uploads build anticipation and keep listeners engaged. Consistency builds habits among listeners, increasing the likelihood of regular downloads and fostering a loyal audience. A regular release schedule will also aid your scheduling and planning, making your workflow more manageable. Consider using a project management tool or content calendar to stay organized.

PLANNING EPISODES

Beyond the format, delve into the detailed planning of each episode. This includes conducting thorough research, outlining a clear structure, and crafting compelling introductions and conclusions. For interview-based episodes, develop a list of insightful and engaging questions. For solo shows, create a detailed script or outline to ensure a cohesive and well-structured presentation. Thorough preparation is key to producing a polished and professional product. And remember to always fact-check your information.

SHOW NOTES

You'll also need to create detailed show notes. Show notes are more than just a list of topics covered in your podcast; they provide valuable context and resources for your listeners. Think of them as an extension of your podcast content, offering supplementary information, links to relevant articles or websites, guest bios, and transcriptions where feasible. Well-written show notes improve listener engagement and demonstrate your dedication to providing a valuable listening experience.

CONSISTENCY

Maintain consistency in style and format across your episodes to establish your podcast's brand identity. Consistent branding builds recognition and helps listeners identify and associate with your content. This applies not just to the audio quality and editing, but also to the overall tone and style of your presentation.

Managing a content calendar effectively will help you maintain a consistent release schedule and organize your workload. Employ a digital calendar, spreadsheet, or dedicated project management tool to track upcoming episodes, deadlines, guest bookings, and promotional activities. This will enhance the efficiency of your podcasting workflow.

If you are collaborating with co-hosts or guests, ensure clear communication and coordination. Establish a collaborative workflow that includes regular communication, shared deadlines, and a clear division of responsibilities. Maintaining open communication channels minimizes potential conflicts and ensures a smooth production process.

One last thought. Consider A/B testing different elements of your podcast to optimize your content strategy. Experiment with different episode formats, release times, and promotional techniques to identify what resonates best with your audience. Monitor your podcast's performance metrics, such as downloads, listener engagement, and feedback, to make data-driven decisions about your content.

Encourage listeners to share their thoughts and suggestions through surveys, social media, or email. Analyze feedback to identify areas for improvement and adapt your content strategy accordingly. Consider incorporating suggestions into future episodes or modifying your approach based on listener preferences.

THE TAKE-AWAY

Continuously analyzing these key elements and adjusting based on data will be pivotal in your journey towards building a successful and engaging podcast. Remember, the continuous refinement of your podcast's content, just like your understanding of your ideal listener, is an ongoing process

5
BUILDING A BRAND IDENTITY FOR YOUR PODCAST

Building a strong brand identity is paramount. Brand identity is more than just a catchy name; it's the overall feeling and impression your podcast leaves on listeners. Think of it as the personality of your show—consistent, memorable, and relatable. This identity encompasses visual elements like your logo and artwork, but also extends to your brand voice, the tone and style of your communication, and the overall experience you offer your listeners.

VISUAL ELEMENTS

First, let's tackle the visual elements. Your podcast logo is the visual shorthand for your brand. It's the first thing potential listeners will see, often on platforms like Apple Podcasts or Spotify. Therefore, it needs to be striking, memorable, and reflective of your podcast's content and tone. Consider hiring a professional graphic designer if you lack design skills. A well-designed logo can communicate your podcast's essence at a glance, creating immediate recognition and appeal. It shouldn't be overly complicated or cluttered. Simplicity and clarity are key to effective logo design. Explore various design styles—minimalist, vintage, modern, illustrative—and choose the style that best aligns with your podcast's personality. Test different versions with your target audience to gather feedback. The feedback will help you fine-tune your design choices to ensure resonance with your intended listeners.

Beyond the logo, your podcast artwork—the cover image for your podcast on various platforms—is equally important. This image serves as the visual representation of your podcast, influencing the decision of potential listeners to subscribe. It needs to be visually appealing and accurately reflect the content and tone of your podcast. High-resolution images ensure clarity across different devices and platforms. Consider using a professional photographer or graphic designer to create visually stunning artwork that captures the essence of your podcast. Make sure the artwork is easily recognizable and easily distinguishable from competitors.

YOUR BRAND VOICE

Your brand voice is the unique style and tone of your communication. It's the way you speak to your listeners, whether through your narration, introductions, interviews, or interactions on social media. Are you formal or informal? Humorous or serious? Authoritative or conversational?

Consistency in your brand voice across all your content helps create a recognizable and trustworthy image for your podcast. Analyze successful podcasts in your niche to identify different brand voices and understand what works well for their audience. Consider including elements of storytelling in your narrative to build a personal connection with your audience. Let your brand voice showcase your own personality while ensuring it's consistent with the overarching theme of your podcast.

PRESENCE AND COMMUNITY

Expanding your brand presence beyond the audio format is mandatory in today's digital landscape. Your podcast shouldn't exist in a vacuum. A dedicated website acts as a central hub for all your podcast-related content. It should include details about your podcast, show notes, episode transcripts, blog posts, guest bios, and contact information. It allows you to provide additional context and resources to your listeners and potentially even offer exclusive content to premium subscribers. Make sure your website is aesthetically pleasing and easy to navigate. It must align perfectly with the visual elements of your brand, ensuring a consistent experience across all platforms.

Social media is another powerful tool to build your brand and engage with your listeners. Create profiles on platforms relevant to your audience—such as X, Instagram, Facebook, TikTok or LinkedIn. Maintain a consistent presence, sharing relevant content, engaging with comments, and interacting with your followers. Use social media to share behind-the-scenes content, create polls and engage listeners in discussions surrounding your podcast's topics.

Use social listening tools to keep track of the online conversations happening around your brand and address any listener concerns promptly. You can use a Google alert to notify you when you're show is mentioned online. Consider scheduling posts in advance using a social media management tool to maintain a regular and impactful presence. Programs such as Hootsuite, Buffer, and Buzzsprout can schedule your episodes and give you data on social shares.

Building a community around your podcast fosters loyalty and creates a space for listeners to connect with each other and with you. Encourage listeners to engage through comments, social media interactions, dedicated online forums, or email. Responding to listener feedback and actively participating in conversations demonstrates your commitment to your audience. Consider creating a Facebook group, a Discord server, or a dedicated subreddit as platforms to foster your online community. This actively promotes community engagement, leading to stronger audience loyalty.

Protecting your intellectual property is another vital aspect of brand building. Consider trademarking your podcast name and logo to safeguard your brand identity. This legal protection prevents others from using your brand name or logo without your permission.

Consult with an intellectual property lawyer to understand the process and ensure proper registration. Furthermore, ensure all your podcast artwork, music, and other content are appropriately licensed or created by you, avoiding any copyright issues. This proactive approach protects your investment and maintains the integrity of your brand.

Analyzing the branding strategies of successful podcasts provides valuable insight. Examine podcasts in your niche and identify those with strong brand identities. Analyze their logos, artwork, website design, and social media presence. Consider what makes their branding effective and how you can adapt those successful elements to your own podcast. Learning from the best-in-class brands will help you develop a winning strategy for your own podcast. Pay attention to how these brands manage their online presence, engage with their audiences, and build community—all vital aspects of successful podcast branding.

The process of building a strong brand identity is an ongoing journey. Continuously evaluate your brand's effectiveness, seek feedback from your listeners, and adapt your strategies as needed.

Regularly review your visual elements, brand voice, and online presence to ensure they remain relevant and engaging. The dynamic nature of the digital landscape requires consistent attention to brand maintenance.

The Take-Away

The more effort you put into building a consistent and engaging brand identity, the more likely it is your podcast will stand out from the crowd and create a thriving community of loyal listeners. A strong brand identity not only attracts ears but also builds lasting relationships.

PART II
THE GEAR

6
CHOOSING THE RIGHT MICROPHONE

Repeat after me: Invest in a good microphone!

Audio quality can make or break an episode. Invest in a decent microphone and sound-proofing measures to ensure crystal-clear audio. While technical perfection might not always be attainable, aiming for professional audio quality demonstrates respect for your guest and your audience. Clear audio enhances the overall listening experience, preventing distractions and keeping the focus on the conversation itself.

In *How to be a Dynamic Podcast Guest and Sell Stuff*, I recommend a Yeti USB mic as a good starter microphone. You can graduate to a higher quality device when your budget allows. That's the takeaway. Here's the detail.

Choosing the right microphone is arguably the most critical decision you'll make when setting up your podcast. Your microphone is the bridge between your voice and your listeners, directly impacting the overall listening experience. A poorly chosen microphone can lead to muffled audio, excessive background noise, and a generally unprofessional sound, potentially driving listeners away. Conversely, a high-quality microphone, properly used, will ensure your podcast sounds polished, clear, and engaging, fostering a more enjoyable listening experience. Let's explore the types of microphones available and the factors to consider when making your selection.

The podcasting world offers three main microphone types: dynamic, condenser, and USB. Each type possesses characteristics that make it better suited for specific recording environments and budgets. Let's delve into the pros and cons of each.

Dynamic Microphones: Known for their robustness and resilience, dynamic microphones are a popular choice for podcasters, especially beginners. Their construction involves a diaphragm that moves in response to sound waves, generating an electrical signal. This design makes them less sensitive to handling noise and more resistant to feedback, ideal for less-than-perfect recording environments. They typically handle high sound pressure levels (SPL) without distortion, making them suitable for loud environments or enthusiastic speakers. Their relative insensitivity also means they're less likely to pick up subtle background noises, which can be a significant advantage in less acoustically treated spaces.

However, dynamic microphones generally have a lower sensitivity compared to condenser microphones. This means they require a stronger audio signal to produce a clear recording. They also don't capture the same level of detail and nuance in the higher frequencies as their condenser counterparts. This can result in a slightly less "warm" or "full" sound, although modern dynamic microphones are constantly improving in this area. For example, the Shure SM7B is a highly regarded dynamic microphone favored by many podcasters for its exceptional clarity and ability to reject background noise. It's a workhorse known for its durability and consistent performance, but it requires a preamplifier due to its lower output level. A more budget-friendly option, the Audio-Technica ATR2100x-USB, is a dynamic USB microphone that offers a good balance of sound quality and affordability, making it a solid choice for those starting out.

Condenser Microphones: Condenser microphones are known for their high sensitivity, capturing a wider range of frequencies and subtle details in your voice. This results in a richer, more detailed, and often warmer sound compared to dynamic microphones. They're especially well-suited for recording in quieter environments where their high sensitivity is an asset, capturing nuances and subtleties that might be missed by a dynamic microphone. Because of this superior frequency response, condenser mics are often preferred for situations requiring high-fidelity audio recording, making them attractive for podcasters who prioritize audio quality.

However, the high sensitivity of condenser microphones is also their Achilles heel. They're more susceptible to picking up background noise, handling noise (the sound of you touching the microphone), and even pops and sibilance (hissing 's' sounds). This necessitates a quieter recording environment and potentially the use of pop filters and shock mounts to minimize unwanted sounds. Furthermore, many condenser microphones require phantom power, meaning they need an audio interface or mixer that can provide this power.

They are generally more fragile than dynamic microphones and need careful handling to avoid damage. Examples of high-quality condenser microphones frequently used in podcasting include the Rode NT1-A, known for its smooth and detailed sound, and the Neumann U 87 Ai, a legendary microphone used in professional studios but significantly more expensive.

USB Microphones: USB microphones offer a convenient all-in-one solution, eliminating the need for separate audio interfaces or phantom power. Many offer surprisingly good sound quality for their price and convenience, making them a popular entry point for new podcasters, or those who are not comfortable with tech.

However, their limited pre-amplification capabilities and sometimes lower frequency response can impact the richness and detail of the audio. While many good USB microphones are available, their sound may not be as flexible or high-fidelity as a separate microphone and audio interface setup. They also tend to lack the same level of versatility; features like XLR connections for future upgrades are absent. The Blue Yeti is a popular USB microphone known for its multiple pickup patterns and decent sound quality for its price, while the Samson Q2U offers both USB and XLR connectivity, providing some flexibility for future expansion.

FACTORS TO CONSIDER IN CHOOSING A MICROPHONE

Beyond the microphone type, several other factors come into play.

Budget: Microphones range from affordable USB options to high-end studio models costing thousands of dollars. Determine how much you're willing to spend before you start your search. But do keep in mind that the investment in a quality microphone is an investment in your podcast's professional quality.

Recording Environment: If your recording space is noisy, a dynamic microphone or a condenser microphone with a tight polar pattern (such as a cardioid) is recommended. For quieter environments, a large-diaphragm condenser microphone will capture more detail. The environment greatly dictates the sensitivity and noise rejection needed from your microphone.

Audio Interface: If you choose a condenser microphone, you'll need an audio interface to provide phantom power. An audio interface also provides additional flexibility for managing sound levels and monitoring.

Desired Audio Quality: If pristine audio quality is your priority, a high-end condenser microphone with a good audio interface will give you the best results. For a more casual podcast, a dynamic or USB microphone might suffice.

Polar Pattern: The polar pattern defines the directionality of the microphone. Cardioid (heart-shaped) patterns are common for podcasting as they focus on sound from the front while minimizing background noise. Omnidirectional patterns capture sound from all directions, while bidirectional patterns capture sound from the front and rear. Choosing the correct polar pattern significantly impacts the quality of your recording.

MICROPHONE PLACEMENT AND NOISE REDUCTION

Even with the best microphone, poor placement can ruin your audio. Position the microphone a few inches from your mouth, and use a pop filter to prevent unwanted pops from explosive consonants (p's and b's).

Additionally, treat your recording environment to minimize background noise.

Sound-absorbing materials like acoustic foam can significantly reduce reflections and echoes. Experiment with microphone placement and use these treatments to find the sweet spot for your recording space.

THE TAKE-AWAY

The ideal microphone for your podcast depends on your specific needs and budget. Consider the pros and cons of dynamic, condenser, and USB microphones, factoring in your recording environment and desired audio quality. Investing time and research in selecting the right microphone will pay off by helping you create a high-quality, engaging podcast that will resonate with your audience. Remember that a good microphone is only one piece of the puzzle; proper microphone technique and post-production processing are also vital to achieving a professional sound. Don't hesitate to experiment and find what works best for your individual needs. Listen to your recordings critically and adjust accordingly. Your ears are your best guide.

7
HEADPHONES AND AUDIO INTERFACES

Repeat after me: Do not rely on your computer speakers. Buy a good set of headphones!

The speakers that come with computers are typically lousy. Even if you've bought external speakers, the feedback and echo issues can sink you. I've used Sony MDR-7506 headphones for years. Decent wireless earbuds can also get the job done and look better if the interview includes video. That's the take-away. Here's the detail.

Headphones and audio interfaces work in tandem to ensure you're capturing and monitoring your audio with the highest possible fidelity. Ignoring their importance can lead to significant problems, from subpar audio quality to missed mistakes that could have been easily corrected during the recording process. Let's examine each in detail.

HEADPHONES

Headphones are your ears during the recording and editing process. They allow you to listen to your audio in real-time, ensuring that your voice is clear, the levels are correct, and there are no unwanted noises creeping into your recording. Choosing the wrong pair can lead to fatigue, inaccurate monitoring, and ultimately, a less-than-stellar final product. There are two main types of headphones relevant to podcasting: open-back and closed-back.

Open-back headphones offer a more natural and spacious soundstage. They allow sound to escape, creating a more immersive listening experience. This can be beneficial during mixing and mastering, allowing you to hear your audio as it would sound on different playback systems. However, this openness also means that sound leaks out, which is a major drawback for podcast recording. If you use open-back headphones while recording, your microphone will likely pick up the sound from your headphones, creating a feedback loop or a muddy, layered audio mess that is extremely difficult to edit. Therefore, open-back headphones are generally better suited for listening to your recordings during editing, rather than during the recording itself. Examples of excellent open-back headphones that are popular amongst audio professionals include the Sennheiser HD 600 and the Audio-Technica ATH-AD700X. These offer exceptional clarity and soundstage without breaking the bank, making them a valuable investment for the post-production phase.

Closed-back headphones, on the other hand, are designed to isolate sound. They prevent sound from leaking out, making them ideal for recording. This is because the sound from your headphones won't be picked up by your microphone, avoiding that dreaded feedback loop. They provide a more accurate representation of your audio as it will be heard by your listeners, since the sound is effectively contained. Closed-back headphones are often slightly less comfortable for extended listening sessions than open-back, as the sound isolation can create a warmer environment within the earcup. However, the trade-off is well worth it for the clarity and precision they provide during recording. Popular closed-back headphone choices for podcasting include the Beyerdynamic DT 770 PRO, known for their durability and accuracy, and the Sony MDR-7506, a long-standing industry standard that's been a reliable staple for many years due to its flat frequency response. Both are robust and comfortable enough for extended recording sessions, offering superior isolation and precise monitoring for avoiding recording errors.

Beyond the open vs. closed-back debate, several other factors should influence your headphone choice. Consider your budget; high-quality headphones can range from a few hundred to several thousand dollars. However, you don't necessarily need the most expensive pair to achieve great results. Many excellent headphones are available at more affordable price points. Look for headphones with a flat frequency response, meaning they don't boost or cut certain frequencies, providing a more accurate representation of your audio. Also, consider comfort; you'll be wearing these for extended periods, so ensure they're comfortable enough for hours of use without causing ear fatigue.

Finally, consider portability and durability. If you record in multiple locations, consider lightweight and easily transportable headphones. Durability is also important, as headphones will face some wear and tear. Look for headphones made from durable materials and with replaceable parts if possible. Investing in a quality pair of headphones is an investment in the quality of your podcast. It is as vital as having a good microphone; you need to be able to monitor what you're recording effectively. Cheap headphones will invariably lead to poor recording quality and may miss key errors that are only picked up by listening more closely.

ANALOG TO DIGITAL - THE AUDIO INTERFACE

Now, let's discuss audio interfaces. An audio interface is a device that connects your microphones and headphones to your computer. While USB microphones offer a simplified setup, a dedicated audio interface offers significantly more control and flexibility. It acts as a bridge, translating the analog audio signals from your microphone into digital signals your computer can understand. This conversion is results in high-quality recording and editing.

Audio interfaces offer several benefits over simply using a USB microphone. First, they typically provide higher quality pre-amps (pre-amplifiers), which boost the signal from your microphone before it reaches your computer. This leads to cleaner, less noisy recordings, particularly advantageous with condenser microphones that require phantom power. Many audio interfaces supply phantom power, a vital component for condenser microphones, which many USB mics lack. An interface also provides multiple inputs, enabling you to connect more than one microphone at a time. This is incredibly useful if you have co-hosts or if you're recording multiple audio sources simultaneously. Furthermore, they often offer better monitoring options, including dedicated headphone outputs with individual volume controls, allowing for precise level adjustments. This feature allows you to carefully monitor each input and make corrections during the recording process.

The quality of the audio interface's Analog-to-Digital Converters (ADCs) and Digital-to-Analog Converters (DACs) is also important. Higher-quality ADCs and DACs result in cleaner audio with a wider dynamic range and improved fidelity. Think of the ADC as capturing the sound, and the DAC as translating it back into the analog sound your headphones reproduce. The better they are, the more detail you can retain in your audio. Good interfaces make the whole process smoother and create a far better audio experience for both the creators and the audience.

When choosing an audio interface, consider your budget and the number of inputs you need. For solo podcasters, a two-input interface is generally sufficient, while those with co-hosts or additional audio sources will require more inputs. Look for interfaces with ASIO drivers (Audio Stream Input/Output), which provide lower latency (delay) for smoother recording and monitoring. Low latency is necessary for a lag-free real-time monitoring experience, preventing frustrating delays that affect your audio workflow. There are many excellent interfaces for podcasters at various price points. The Focusrite Scarlett Solo is a popular and budget-friendly option for solo podcasters, while the Focusrite Scarlett 2i2 provides two inputs, suitable for co-hosted podcasts. For professional-level recording, interfaces from brands like Universal Audio or RME offer superior quality but come with a significantly higher price tag.

Connecting your audio interface to your computer is usually straightforward. Most interfaces use USB connectivity, but some use Thunderbolt for faster data transfer. Once connected, install the necessary drivers provided by the manufacturer. Then, configure your audio settings within your recording software to select the audio interface as your input and output device. This process ensures the sound from your microphone is routed through the interface, not through your computer's built-in sound card.

The Take-Away

Investing in quality headphones and an audio interface is a significant step towards creating a professional-sounding podcast. Remember, clear audio monitoring is essential for both recording and editing. Choose headphones suited to your recording and editing workflows, prioritizing comfort and accurate sound reproduction. Select an audio interface that meets your needs in terms of inputs and features, focusing on quality pre-amps and low-latency drivers. By carefully considering these aspects of your podcast setup, you'll greatly enhance the overall quality and professionalism of your podcast production, making it a more enjoyable listening experience for your audience. The investment pays off tenfold when you consider the resulting audio quality.

Don't skimp these important parts of your podcast setup; the end result will be a noticeable improvement.

8
SETTING UP YOUR RECORDING SPACE

Fix the Room!

Now that we've established the importance of high-quality microphones, headphones, and audio interfaces, let's turn our attention to the most often overlooked, yet critically important aspect of podcast production: your recording environment. The quality of your recording space directly impacts the final audio quality, regardless of how expensive your equipment is. A poorly treated room can introduce unwanted noises, echoes, and reverberation, completely undermining the clarity and professionalism of even the best microphones and audio interfaces.

Creating an acoustically treated recording space is an investment that pays significant dividends. While a professional recording studio offers optimal conditions, most podcasters operate from home studios, making careful room treatment paramount. The goal is to minimize background noise and unwanted reflections, creating a more controlled and consistent sound. This section will guide you through the process of setting up a suitable recording space, whether you're working with a dedicated room or repurposing a corner of your home.

The first step is to assess your current recording environment.

Identify potential sources of noise. This might include traffic noise, HVAC systems, neighboring apartments, or even household appliances like refrigerators or washing machines. Note the location of reflective surfaces such as windows, hard floors, and bare walls.

These surfaces bounce sound waves around the room, causing echoes and reverberation, making your audio sound muddy and unprofessional.

Once you've identified the problem areas, you can start to address them. The most effective method is to use sound-absorbing materials. These materials are designed to absorb sound waves, reducing reflections and minimizing reverberation. Commonly used materials include acoustic panels, bass traps, and diffusion panels.

Acoustic panels are typically made from foam or other porous materials and are readily available online and at music stores. They come in various thicknesses and sizes, offering different levels of absorption. Thicker panels generally absorb lower frequencies better. Experimentation is key here; you might find a combination of panels with varying thicknesses achieves the best results in your specific space. Consider strategically placing them on walls behind your microphone and on any reflective surfaces facing it. Don't be afraid to cover significant wall space; you want to dampen the room's natural echo.

Bass traps are designed to absorb low-frequency sounds, which are notorious for causing booming or muddy audio. These frequencies are often problematic because they are difficult to absorb with standard acoustic panels. Bass traps are usually placed in corners, where low-frequency sound waves tend to accumulate. There are various types of bass traps, from professionally manufactured units to DIY solutions using rockwool or mineral wool, which offer excellent sound absorption, as long as they are properly enclosed and covered.

Diffusion panels, unlike absorption panels, don't absorb sound; they scatter it. This is particularly helpful for breaking up standing waves, which are stationary sound waves that can cause undesirable resonant frequencies in a room. Diffusion panels are often used in conjunction with acoustic panels to create a more balanced and natural-sounding environment. They help prevent the audio from sounding too "dead" and enhance acoustic clarity.

Beyond panels, other readily available materials can enhance sound absorption. Thick carpets or rugs on hard floors significantly reduce reflections. Heavy curtains or drapes can also help absorb sound and dampen reflections from windows. Furniture, particularly upholstered pieces, also help absorb sound. Strategically placing furniture can aid in creating a more controlled acoustic environment.

However, simply adding sound-absorbing materials isn't a one-size-fits-all solution. The size and shape of your room will influence the placement and type of materials you need. For instance, a small room might require fewer panels than a larger room to achieve the same level of acoustic treatment. Consider the size and dimensions of your room. Experiment with the placement of sound-absorbing materials to find the optimal arrangement.

For budget-friendly solutions, consider using readily available materials like thick blankets or moving boxes filled with clothes or other sound-absorbing materials. While not as aesthetically pleasing as professionally made panels, these can be effective in dampening reflections. Remember, the goal is to minimize the room's resonance to keep the recordings clean.

In addition to material selection and placement, It's important to locate the best position for your microphone within the room. Experiment, moving the microphone a few inches or feet at a time to find the "sweet spot," where the sound is the clearest and most free of reflections. Listen critically to recordings made at different positions to identify areas where reflections are less noticeable. This often involves avoiding close proximity to walls or hard surfaces.

For those with a dedicated recording space, investing in professional acoustic treatment is worth the consideration. Many professional soundproofing techniques go far beyond simply adding panels. This can involve things like adding insulation to walls, sealing gaps and cracks that allow sound to leak through, and using specialized soundproof doors and windows. However, these professional-level techniques represent a considerable investment in terms of both time and money. Start with the readily available and easily implemented solutions first to gain an understanding of your specific recording environment before moving into more advanced and expensive options.

Creating the ideal recording environment is a process of trial and error. Listen critically to your recordings as you adjust your setup. Experiment with different microphone positions, sound-absorbing materials, and room layouts. The more experimentation you do, the better you'll be able to find the optimal setup for your specific needs. Remember that even a modest investment in acoustic treatment can dramatically improve the quality of your podcast. Invest time in experimenting with your sound-treating options to find the best balance between controlling reverberations and maintaining a natural acoustic. The investment in a well-treated recording space will enhance the professional quality of your recordings and provide listeners with a far more enjoyable listening experience. The clearer, cleaner sound will make all the difference in your podcast's overall success.

Beyond acoustic treatment, consider the overall ambiance of your recording space. A comfortable and quiet environment will help you relax and deliver your best performance. Make sure the room is well-lit and adequately temperature-controlled. Clutter can create a distracting atmosphere, so keep your recording area organized and tidy. A clear, quiet environment, free from distractions, helps in producing clean, high-quality audio recordings.

THE TAKE-AWAY

Setting up a well-treated recording space is a critical step in elevating the professional quality of your podcast. This process involves assessing your current environment, identifying noise sources and reflective surfaces, and strategically using sound-absorbing materials to minimize reflections and reverberation. Remember to experiment with different materials, placements, and microphone positions to optimize your setup. While professional-level soundproofing can be expensive, readily available and cost-effective methods can deliver significant improvements in audio quality. This investment in your recording environment will directly translate to a superior listening experience for your audience, enhancing the overall impact and professionalism of your podcast. The improvements will be well worth the effort.

9
AN INTRODUCTION TO AUDIO EDITING SOFTWARE

Fix it in post.

One of the biggest cliches in motion pictures is the term "fix it in post." This refers to sharpening the finished product after the shooting is done. From an efficiency standpoint, the more you can do to avoid having to edit afterwards gives you the time to do all the other things we'll talk about. But there will be instances where you will want to remove some blemishes, or perhaps do major surgery to turn a potential disaster into a winner.

Since the scope of this book primarily focuses on audio podcasting, lets delve into the tools that help you edit the show. This is where the magic truly happens, transforming raw recordings into polished, professional-sounding podcasts. While a well-treated recording space significantly reduces post-production work, audio editing remains a key step in creating a high-quality podcast. This involves the use of audio editing software to refine your recordings, correct imperfections, and enhance the overall listening experience.

As this book is being written, the power of artificial intelligence is being harnessed to create editable transcripts within the podcast recording applications. This lets you cut, paste and in some instances re-voice pieces of your podcast without leaving the website where you recorded the show. Descript and Riverside are two examples of podcast recording platforms that facilitate this. The functionality will only improve and there may come a day where the outboard audio editors we will discuss might become dinosaurs. Learning how to select and use powerful software is still necessary. So lets explore two popular and widely used options: Audacity (a free, open-source program) and Adobe Audition (a professional-grade, subscription-based software). Understanding the capabilities and limitations of each will help you choose the software that best suits your needs and budget. While many other excellent options exist, focusing on these two provides a comprehensive overview, ranging from beginner-friendly tools to more sophisticated options for advanced users.

Audacity: The free alternative with a learning curve

Let's start with Audacity, a remarkably versatile and accessible piece of software. Its open-source nature means it's entirely free to download and use, making it an ideal choice for aspiring podcasters on a budget. Despite its free status, Audacity offers a surprising range of features, capable of handling most common editing tasks with ease. The interface, while perhaps not as visually polished as some commercial alternatives, is intuitive and straightforward, allowing even beginners to quickly grasp the basics.

Upon opening Audacity, you're greeted with a clean workspace. At the top, you'll find the menu bar, offering access to all the software's functions. Below this is the toolbar, providing quick access to commonly used tools like play, record, pause, stop, and undo/redo. The main area displays the waveform of your audio file– a visual representation of the sound, showing its amplitude and frequency over time. This visual representation is critical for precise editing. The bottom panel typically displays the timeline, allowing you to precisely navigate through your recording.

One of Audacity's most valuable features is its extensive library of effects. These effects allow you to manipulate your audio in various ways, from basic noise reduction and equalization to more advanced functions like compression and reverb. Let's take a closer look at some editing techniques commonly used in podcast production.

Noise reduction is perhaps the most important editing function. Even in a well-treated room, minor background noises might creep into your recordings. Audacity's noise reduction tool helps minimize these unwanted sounds without significantly affecting the quality of your voice or other audio elements. The process typically involves selecting a portion of the audio containing only background noise, then applying the noise reduction effect. Audacity analyzes this section and creates a noise profile, which it then uses to filter out similar noises throughout the rest of the recording. Experimentation is key; you'll likely need to adjust the noise reduction settings to find the optimal balance between noise reduction and preserving the audio quality.

Audio leveling is another critical step. Ensuring consistent volume levels throughout your recording contributes to a professional sound. Audacity provides tools to normalize your audio, bringing quieter parts up to a consistent level and reducing the loudness of excessively loud sections. This creates a more even listening experience, avoiding abrupt volume changes that can disrupt the flow. Audacity also offers compression, a more sophisticated technique for controlling the dynamic range of your audio, preventing loud sections from being too jarring and quiet parts from being too faint.

Beyond these fundamental tools, Audacity allows for more advanced editing, such as cutting, pasting, and splicing audio sections, adding fade-ins and fade-outs for smoother transitions, and even incorporating sound effects. It's important to use these tools judiciously; overuse of sound effects can detract from the overall quality and professionalism of your podcast. The goal is subtle enhancement, not overt manipulation. Audacity provides the tools for both, empowering you to choose the right balance.

Adobe Audition: The pro's choice

Now, let's shift our focus to Adobe Audition, a more powerful and feature-rich software. Audition is a professional-grade audio workstation, providing a comprehensive suite of tools for advanced audio editing and manipulation. It offers a more sophisticated interface, featuring multiple panels and windows for managing various aspects of your audio project. While the learning curve is steeper than Audacity's, the advanced features justify the increased complexity.

Audition boasts a powerful noise reduction tool, often considered superior to Audacity's in its ability to selectively remove background noise without affecting the desired audio. It utilizes more sophisticated algorithms to analyze and remove noise, minimizing artifacts and preserving audio fidelity. Audition's advanced features extend beyond noise reduction; it includes advanced equalization, compression, and mastering tools, often found in professional music production software.

Audition excels in its multitrack editing capabilities, enabling you to work with multiple audio tracks simultaneously. This is extremely useful for podcasts involving multiple speakers, music, or sound effects. You can easily arrange and adjust individual tracks, creating a more polished and layered sound. Audition also offers advanced tools for restoring and repairing damaged audio, such as removing clicks, pops, and other imperfections. This is particularly helpful if you're working with older recordings or recordings with inherent flaws.

However, Adobe Audition's sophistication comes at a cost. It's a subscription-based software, requiring a recurring payment to access its features. This cost might be prohibitive for beginners or those with tighter budgets. Furthermore, its more complex interface may initially prove daunting for users unfamiliar with professional audio editing software.

The choice between Audacity and Adobe Audition ultimately depends on your specific needs, technical skills, and budget.

Audacity is the ideal starting point for beginners, offering a user-friendly environment and a powerful set of tools without the cost.

Once you've gained experience and your podcasting ambitions

grow, Audition might become a necessary upgrade, offering the professional-grade tools needed to create truly exceptional audio.

Both programs provide ample tutorials and online resources to guide you through the learning process, ensuring you're comfortable with the software's capabilities.

Mastering audio editing is a journey, not a destination. Begin by mastering the basics, focusing on noise reduction, leveling, and clean transitions. As your skills grow, explore more advanced techniques to refine your podcast's overall sound. Experimentation and practice are key; the more you use the software, the more comfortable and adept you'll become, ultimately creating a significantly enhanced listening experience for your audience.

A well-edited podcast conveys professionalism, enhancing credibility and ensuring a more enjoyable experience for your listeners.

MASTERING YOUR PODCAST AUDIO

Now that we've explored the basics of audio editing using Audacity and Adobe Audition, we can move on to the all important stage of audio mastering. Mastering isn't just about making your podcast louder; it's about optimizing the overall sound quality, ensuring a consistent and professional listening experience. This involves a series of processes designed to polish your audio, making it suitable for distribution across various platforms. Think of it as the final polish on a finely crafted piece of art.

The first step in mastering is audio normalization. Normalization adjusts the volume levels of your audio file, ensuring that the overall loudness is consistent from beginning to end. This prevents jarring volume spikes or drops that can disrupt the listening experience. Many editing programs automatically offer normalization, but you should always visually inspect your waveform to ensure that the levels are smooth and even. Uneven volume is a common issue in poorly mastered podcasts and can be very distracting to the listener.

Aim for a consistent peak level, avoiding clipping (distortion caused by exceeding the maximum amplitude).

Next comes compression. Compression reduces the dynamic range of your audio, bringing down loud peaks and boosting quieter parts.

This results in a more even and balanced sound, particularly beneficial for podcasts with varying levels of speech volume, such as those featuring interviews or multiple speakers. Careful compression enhances clarity and prevents listeners from needing to constantly adjust their volume. Over-compression, however, can result in a lifeless and unnatural sound, losing the natural dynamics of the voices and music. The key is finding the right balance; experimentation is required in order to achieve a natural, yet consistent sound.

Equalization, or EQ, is another important part of mastering. EQ allows you to adjust the balance of different frequencies in your audio, boosting certain frequencies while attenuating others. This can be used to enhance clarity, remove muddiness, and create a more polished sound. For instance, you might boost the higher frequencies to make vocals sound clearer and crisper, or reduce low-end rumble to eliminate any unwanted background noise. EQ is a powerful tool, but it requires a careful ear. Excessive EQ can result in an unnatural and unpleasant sound, so make subtle adjustments. Remember to listen critically and adjust accordingly – less is often more. You can use visual cues in the audio editing software's spectrum analyzer to identify frequencies requiring adjustments.

Limiting is the final step in mastering, placing a ceiling on the maximum loudness of your audio. Limiting prevents clipping and ensures that your podcast sounds consistently loud across different platforms and devices. While increasing loudness is tempting, avoid over-limiting, which can result in a harsh, compressed sound. The goal is to maximize loudness without sacrificing audio quality. A well-mastered podcast will sound powerful yet still retain its natural dynamics. Proper limiting ensures your podcast is loud enough to compete favorably with others but maintains clarity and avoids distortion.

Mastering also involves careful attention to detail. This includes removing any unwanted clicks, pops, or other artifacts that might have slipped through the editing process. A good audio mastering technique involves eliminating any stray noises or distracting sounds, ensuring the final product is as clean and polished as possible. Careful listening during this process can significantly improve the overall quality. This is where your trained ear becomes invaluable; you should be listening for any inconsistencies or imperfections that might detract from the listening experience.

Let's delve into some practical examples of good and bad podcast audio mastering. A poorly mastered podcast will often have fluctuating volume levels, causing the listener to constantly adjust their device's volume control. The sound might be muddled or lack clarity, making it difficult to understand the speaker. Excessive background noise or pops and clicks might also be noticeable, detracting from the overall listening experience. In contrast, a well-mastered podcast will feature consistent volume levels, clear and articulate audio, and minimal background noise. The sound will be balanced, allowing the listener to fully focus on the content without distractions.

In a podcast setting, poor mastering might leave the interviewer's voice much louder than the interviewee's, creating an imbalance and making one voice difficult to hear. Conversely, good mastering will ensure both voices are clearly audible and at similar volume levels, creating a smooth and balanced listening experience. The use of compression will also help to ensure a consistent sound, smoothing out any sudden peaks or dips in volume.

Another important aspect of mastering is considering the different platforms where your podcast will be distributed. Each platform has its own specifications and guidelines regarding loudness and audio quality. For instance, some platforms might automatically normalize or compress your audio, potentially affecting the final product if it's already heavily processed. Therefore, you should aim for a balanced and professional-sounding master that will translate well across all platforms.

One common pitfall in audio mastering is over-processing. Trying to make your audio "perfect" through excessive compression, equalization, or limiting can often result in a lifeless and unnatural sound. The audio might lack dynamic range, making it feel flat and uninteresting. Remember, the goal of mastering is to enhance the audio, not to drastically alter it. Strive for a natural and balanced sound, focusing on improving clarity, consistency, and loudness, but without artificial enhancements.

Another frequent mistake is neglecting the importance of a consistent listening environment when mastering. You should ideally master your audio in a properly treated room, using high-quality monitoring equipment. This ensures you accurately hear the subtle nuances in your audio and make appropriate adjustments. Using poor-quality headphones or speakers can lead to inaccurate adjustments, resulting in a poorly mastered final product. The mastering environment should be acoustically neutral to allow you to hear a clear representation of the sound without room reflections affecting your judgment.

THE TAKE-AWAY

Learning how to use your tools is an ongoing process. It's rarely a one-and-done situation. You might need to adjust levels, EQ, and compression multiple times until you achieve the desired result.

Don't be afraid to experiment; listen critically and make adjustments based on what you hear. You'll find that the more you practice, the better you'll become at mastering your podcasts.

PART III
THE ART OF THE INTERVIEW

10
LUCK FAVORS THE PREPARED

Planning and preparing for interviews is arguably the most critical aspect of creating a successful podcast. A well-prepared interview flows naturally, elicits insightful responses, and keeps the listener engaged. This preparation goes far beyond simply compiling a list of questions; it involves a thorough understanding of your guest, their expertise, and your overall podcast goals.

The first step is thorough research. Before even contacting a potential guest, you need to understand their background, their work, and their perspective on relevant topics. This involves more than just a cursory glance at their website or LinkedIn profile. Dive deep into their publications, their past interviews, and their online presence to identify key themes, recurring ideas, and areas where they possess insights. Understanding their body of work allows you to formulate questions that are both relevant and insightful, leading to a more engaging and informative conversation.

For example, if interviewing a historian specializing in the American Civil War, a simple question like "Tell us about the Civil War" is far too broad. Instead, after researching their specific area of expertise (perhaps focusing on the economic aspects of the war in the South), you might ask, "Your recent work on the Southern economy during the Civil War suggests a complex relationship between plantation owners and the Confederacy. Can you elaborate on how financial pressures influenced strategic decisions within the Confederate leadership?" This targeted question demonstrates your understanding of their work and invites a nuanced response, enriching the listening experience for your audience.

This research also extends to identifying any potential points of conflict or controversy within their work. Being aware of these sensitivities allows you to navigate the conversation with tact and respect, avoiding uncomfortable silences or potentially contentious exchanges. A respectful and informed approach establishes trust and encourages the guest to open up, fostering a more genuine and productive interview.

Once you've thoroughly researched your guest, it's time to create an interview outline. This outline isn't a rigid script; instead, it serves as a flexible guide to ensure you cover key topics.

Categorize your questions into logical themes, allowing for a natural progression of the conversation. Begin with broader, introductory questions to establish context and build rapport before moving into more specific and detailed inquiries. Remember to include a few open-ended questions that encourage the guest to share their insights and perspectives freely. These questions can spark spontaneous and engaging conversations.

For instance, you could start with a general question about the guest's work and then progressively drill down into specifics. Imagine interviewing a software developer about their latest app. You could begin with "Can you describe the genesis of your latest app and what problem it solves?" This broad question leads into more specific follow-ups like, "What were the most challenging aspects of the development process?", and "What were some innovative solutions you implemented to overcome these challenges?" The progression from general to specific ensures a smooth and structured conversation, preventing jarring transitions between topics.

Next, you must contact your guest. Clearly outline the purpose of the interview, the anticipated length, the topics to be discussed, and the desired date and time. Attach your podcast's website or social media links to provide the guest with context and build credibility. Be respectful of their time and provide ample flexibility in scheduling. Remember, securing the interview is a collaborative effort, not a one-sided demand. Follow up if you haven't received a response within a reasonable timeframe. Maintain polite and professional communication throughout the entire process.

After securing your guest's participation, refine your interview questions based on any further information they provide. This back-and-forth communication helps to personalize the conversation and ensures its relevance. A strong relationship between interviewer and interviewee will often lead to a more productive and engaging interview.

Furthermore, consider the broader context of your podcast's audience. Tailor questions to address the interests and knowledge level of your listeners. Avoid using highly technical jargon or overly specialized terminology without providing adequate explanation. The goal is to make the information accessible and engaging for a broad audience, not just for experts in the field.

THE TAKE-AWAY

Effective interviewing requires meticulous planning and preparation. By thoroughly researching your guest, outlining insightful questions, and developing strong communication skills, you can create a dynamic, informative, and engaging podcast episode. Remember that preparation translates to a smoother workflow during the interview, fostering a more collaborative and productive conversation. The time and effort invested in the pre-interview process ultimately enhances the quality of your podcast and ensures a richer listening experience for your audience.

11
HOW TO TALK TO PEOPLE—ASKING EFFECTIVE QUESTIONS AND MANAGING THE FLOW

Building upon the groundwork of preparation, the next element in crafting a compelling podcast interview lies in conducting engaging and informative conversations. This goes beyond simply asking pre-prepared questions; it's about fostering a dynamic exchange, drawing out the guest's expertise, and making the interview both insightful for the listener and enjoyable for all involved.

Begin the interview with a brief, informal exchange to build rapport. A few casual questions about the guest's travel or any recent experience can help them feel at ease before you delve into the more substantive topics. Remember, the goal is to have a conversation, not an interrogation. The more relaxed the guest feels, the more openly and honestly they'll share their insights.

The cornerstone of any successful interview is the art of questioning. While your research will have provided a robust foundation, the actual conversation requires adaptability and finesse. Open-ended questions—those that don't have simple "yes" or "no" answers, prompt deeper explanations and personal reflections. For instance, instead of asking a novelist, "Did you enjoy writing your new book?", try "What were the most rewarding and challenging aspects of crafting your latest novel?" This invites a richer response, potentially revealing insights into the creative process, struggles overcome, and the author's personal journey.

Equally important are follow-up questions. These aren't merely repetitions; they're strategic probes that delve deeper into interesting points raised by the guest. If a guest mentions a specific challenge in their field, a follow-up could be, "Can you elaborate on that challenge? What specific strategies did you employ to overcome it?" This demonstrates active listening and encourages a more detailed explanation, providing the audience with a more comprehensive understanding.

Active listening is not just about hearing the words; it's about engaging with the meaning behind them. This involves fully concentrating on what the guest is saying, both verbally and nonverbally. Pay attention to their tone, their body language, and the nuances of their expression. This attentiveness will enable you to ask more pertinent follow-up questions, demonstrating to the guest that you are truly invested in their perspective. Verbal cues like "That's a fascinating point," "I see," or "Tell me more about that," reinforce your active participation and encourage the guest to continue sharing their thoughts.

However, even the best-laid plans can encounter unexpected challenges. Some guests might be naturally reserved or hesitant to open up. In these situations, patience and empathy are vital. Give them time to adjust to the interview setting and gently guide the conversation towards more comfortable territory. Offer positive reinforcement and acknowledge their contributions, even if they're brief. Consider incorporating visual cues if the interview is conducted remotely, a simple nod or smile can encourage participation. Remember, the goal is to facilitate a comfortable exchange; forcing a response is counterproductive.

Unexpected tangents are another common occurrence. A guest might veer off-topic, sharing an interesting anecdote or diverging into a related but tangential discussion. While these diversions can sometimes lead to unexpected insights, you'll need to be able to guide the conversation back to the main theme at the appropriate time. Employ smooth transitions such as, "That's a fascinating story, but let's return to our discussion on [main topic]," or "We'll have to explore that in more detail another time, but for now, let's focus on [main topic]."

Such redirection should be polite and subtle, maintaining a conversational flow instead of abruptly interrupting. It's a delicate balance; you want to encourage genuine interaction without losing focus. The pre-interview preparation, with a well-defined structure, makes this redirection easier and more natural.

Maintaining a consistent conversational pace can keep listeners engaged. Avoid long, monotonous monologues, whether from yourself or your guest. Break up the conversation with shorter, more concise segments. If you sense a lull in the conversation, employ your prepared backup questions, or use a strategic pause to encourage the guest to elaborate on a particular point. This controlled pacing helps maintain audience attention and prevents the interview from feeling flat.

Handling difficult or unexpected situations requires a blend of preparedness, adaptability, and tact. If a guest unexpectedly contradicts themself or offers information that challenges your prior knowledge, resist the urge to immediately correct them. Instead, politely acknowledge their statement and then subtly guide the conversation towards a clearer understanding. You could say something like, "That's an interesting perspective. Could you elaborate on that point, perhaps by giving us a concrete example?" Or, "I'm interested in understanding how you reconcile that with your earlier point about [specific topic]." This approach encourages self-correction without making them feel challenged or defensive.

Remember, the goal is not to "win" the interview or prove your knowledge, but to facilitate a meaningful exchange of information. Your role as the interviewer is to guide the conversation, draw out insightful perspectives, and ensure that the information is presented in a clear and engaging manner for the audience. Be patient, attentive, and respectful, and the conversation will naturally flow, resulting in a truly enriching podcast experience.

Beyond the specific techniques, a significant factor in conducting engaging interviews is your own personality and communication style. While preparation is important, genuine enthusiasm and a natural conversational approach are equally vital. Let your personality shine through; your genuine interest in the guest and their expertise will be infectious.

WHEN TECH GOES WRONG

Unexpected technical glitches are an ever-present threat in the world of remote podcasting, and can derail even the most meticulously planned interviews. These can range from dropped calls and internet connectivity issues to microphone malfunctions and software glitches. Having a backup plan is crucial. This includes having alternate communication methods (e.g., a secondary phone line or video conferencing platform) readily available. It's also important to have backup equipment, such as a spare microphone or headphones.

Before starting the interview, conduct a thorough technical check with the guest, ensuring all systems are working correctly and everyone understands the procedure for addressing technical glitches. During the interview, maintain a calm and reassuring demeanor, assuring your guest that you'll resolve the issue quickly and efficiently.

Handling interruptions—whether it's unexpected noises, intrusions from other people, or even a sudden power outage—is a necessary skill. If the interruption is brief, acknowledging it with a brief comment, such as, "Excuse me for a moment," and promptly resolving it maintains professionalism and minimizes disruption to the flow. For more significant interruptions, be prepared to pause the recording, address the issue, and resume the conversation smoothly, perhaps even using it as an opportunity for a brief humorous anecdote if appropriate. Maintaining a relaxed yet controlled atmosphere reassures both the guest and the audience that you are in control.

POST-INTERVIEW ANALYSIS

Post-interview, review your recording and identify potential areas for improvement. Did you ask every question you planned? Did the conversation flow smoothly? Did you provide sufficient context for the listeners? Reflecting on these areas will help refine your interviewing skills over time.

12
POST INTERVIEW EDITING AND PRODUCTION

Post-interview editing is where the magic truly happens, transforming raw audio into a polished, engaging podcast episode. This process involves more than just cutting out mistakes; it's about shaping the narrative, enhancing the listening experience, and ensuring your guest's message is conveyed accurately and effectively. Think of it as the final polish on a finely crafted piece of jewelry – attention to detail is paramount.

The first stage is audio cleanup. This involves addressing any background noise, such as traffic, hums from electronics, or the ever-present air conditioner. Software like Audacity or Adobe Audition offer powerful noise reduction tools. These tools utilize algorithms to identify and minimize unwanted sounds without significantly affecting the quality of your guest's voice. The key is finding the right balance. Too much noise reduction can result in a thin, unnatural sound, while too little leaves the listener distracted by ambient noises. Experimentation is key; you'll quickly develop an ear for what sounds best. Often, a combination of noise reduction and equalization (EQ) proves most effective. EQ allows you to boost or cut certain frequencies, enhancing clarity and bringing out specific aspects of the audio.

As this book was being written, the on-line Adobe Sound Enhancer was becoming the gold standard for voice enhancement. It is a feature which comes with the Creative Suite that includes Audition and lets you drag and drop your interview file onto a page where magic in the cloud truly transforms every voice, eliminating room noise, adjusting for poor microphones and giving your conversation a true broadcast feel.

Removing unwanted sounds is equally important. This includes coughs, sneezes, misplaced words, or any other interruptions that occurred during the interview. While aiming for minimal editing, completely eliminating extraneous sounds can dramatically improve the listener experience. This process often requires precision and patience. You'll need to listen carefully, identify the offending sounds, and then surgically remove them without impacting the surrounding audio. Here's where familiarity with your chosen editing software's tools can really help you—mastering techniques like cross-fading and using selection tools will make this process much more efficient.

Beyond noise reduction, post-interview editing is about enhancing clarity and flow. This involves adjusting audio levels, ensuring the guest's voice is consistently loud and clear throughout the interview. You might need to normalize the audio to bring all sections to a consistent volume, preventing sudden jumps in loudness. If the conversation lagged in certain areas, you can strategically edit out moments of silence or awkward pauses, maintaining a steady pace that keeps listeners engaged. However, remember that removing too much can render the conversation unnatural. The goal is to enhance, not to manufacture, a smooth and seamless narrative.

Respecting your guest's voice is absolutely critical. The editing process shouldn't change the meaning or intent of their statements.

Avoid taking things out of context or manipulating their words to fit a narrative that wasn't originally there. Ethical considerations are at the forefront of this stage. Your goal is to present your guest accurately and authentically. Any edits made should be subtle and transparent, enhancing the overall listening experience without compromising the integrity of the interview. If you're unsure about a particular edit, it's always better to err on the side of caution and leave it in.

Assembling the final interview audio involves more than just stringing together the edited sections. It's a matter of crafting a cohesive whole. This process includes adding your introduction and outro segments. These act as bookends, setting the stage for the interview and providing context for the listener. These segments should be concise and engaging, quickly orienting the listener to the topic and the guest. They should also maintain the overall tone and style of the podcast. Consider incorporating a catchy intro/outro music or sound effects, which can significantly enhance the listener's experience.

Beyond the technical skills, there's an art to post-interview editing. It requires a keen ear for detail, a sense of timing and pacing, and a creative eye for enhancing the overall listening experience. You're not just cleaning up audio; you're crafting a narrative, shaping the conversation, and ensuring your guest's voice is heard clearly and effectively. This process requires patience, practice, and attention to detail. The results, however, are well worth the effort—a polished, engaging podcast episode that captivates your audience and showcases your skill as a producer. This translates into a superior listener experience, and more importantly, a significant increase in credibility and trust.

Remember, your goal is to create a seamless and engaging listening experience. The editing process shouldn't be noticeable to the listener – it should be invisible, enhancing the natural flow and clarity of the conversation. This requires a delicate balance between removing distractions and preserving the authenticity of the interview. By mastering these techniques, you'll not only create high-quality podcasts but also enhance your skills as a storyteller.

This translates into greater audience engagement and a stronger connection with your listeners. As your experience grows, your editing prowess will only improve, reflecting in the quality of your podcast episodes and demonstrating a commitment to excellence in audio production.

THE TAKE-AWAY

The post-production process extends beyond mere technical proficiency; it involves critical listening skills, a keen understanding of narrative structure, and a commitment to ethical representation. Your goal is to enhance the guest's message, not to manipulate it. Every click, every fade, every subtle adjustment should contribute to the overall quality and impact of the final product. This blend of technical expertise and artistic sensibility sets apart truly exceptional podcasts, establishing a clear connection between the producer and their audience. Through careful editing, you transform raw interview audio into a compelling, polished piece of audio storytelling, showcasing both your guest's expertise and your skills as a dedicated audio professional. This meticulous attention to detail elevates your podcast, creating a distinctive listening experience for your loyal audience and attracting new listeners with the high-quality production. This attention to post-production details speaks volumes about your commitment to quality and professional standing.

13

WHAT ABOUT MUSIC AND SOUND EFFECTS?

While compelling content is the bedrock of any successful podcast, the skillful integration of audio elements can significantly enhance the listening experience, boosting engagement and leaving a lasting impression on your audience. This isn't about simply throwing in some background music; it's a carefully considered process of selecting, licensing, and implementing sounds to complement your narrative, create mood, and guide the listener's journey.

The first step involves understanding the different roles music and sound effects can play in your podcast. Music, for instance, can set the tone. A driving, upbeat track might be ideal for an energetic news commentary, while a mellow, acoustic piece could better suit a reflective interview. Sound effects, on the other hand, serve a more functional purpose, often used to punctuate key moments, transition between segments, or add subtle layers of depth and realism. The sound of a crackling fire might enhance a storytelling podcast, while the gentle tick-tock of a clock could create suspense in a true crime narrative. The key is to choose sounds that are appropriate for your content and enhance, not distract from, your message.

However, the use of music and sound effects isn't simply about artistic expression; it carries significant legal and ethical considerations. Copyright infringement is a real risk, particularly for podcasters who use commercially licensed music without proper authorization. Using copyrighted material without permission can lead to legal action, costly penalties, and the removal of your podcast from hosting platforms. Therefore, understanding copyright law and acquiring the necessary licenses is paramount.

Fortunately, many resources offer royalty-free music and sound effects. These resources provide access to a vast library of audio clips that can be used in your podcast without fear of copyright infringement. Websites like PremiumBeat, Epidemic Sound, and Artlist offer subscriptions that provide access to a wide range of high-quality music suitable for various moods and genres. For sound effects, consider websites like Freesound.org, which offers a vast community-driven library of free-to-use audio clips. Remember to always check the license associated with each audio element, as terms and conditions can vary.

The process of incorporating music and sound effects into your podcast requires careful planning and execution. It's not just a matter of dragging and dropping audio files into your editing software; it's about creating a seamless and balanced soundscape that complements your narration and enhances the overall listening experience. For instance, music should generally be kept at a lower volume than your voice to avoid masking your dialogue. Sound effects should be used sparingly and strategically, to highlight specific moments or transitions, and should never overpower the rest of the audio.

Consider the use of fades and crossfades to avoid jarring transitions between music, sound effects, and dialogue. Smooth transitions create a more professional and polished sound. Use EQ and compression to blend the different audio elements and ensure a consistent overall sound quality. Remember to maintain a balance in your audio mix. Avoid overwhelming your listeners with excessive music or sound effects; less is often more. The goal is to enhance, not overshadow, the main focus of your podcast, which is your content and your voice.

Experiment with different techniques to find what works best for your podcast. For instance, you could use a consistent theme song to introduce each episode, creating a sense of branding and familiarity for your listeners. Or you could use subtle background music to create atmosphere during interviews or storytelling segments. The possibilities are limitless, and experimentation is encouraged, but always keep your audience's experience at the forefront of your decisions.

Let's look at some practical examples. Imagine a podcast that discusses historical events. The use of period-appropriate music during segments describing a specific historical event could greatly enhance the listener's immersion and understanding. Sound effects, such as the clash of swords or the sounds of a bustling city, could add realistic texture to the narrative. However, using too many sound effects could be jarring and overwhelming. The key is to use them judiciously, enhancing the story without distracting from it.

Conversely, a podcast about personal finance could benefit from calm and reassuring background music during segments addressing anxieties surrounding money. The use of gentle, repetitive sounds could create a sense of stability and control. However, overly energetic or upbeat music might be inappropriate in such a setting, potentially undermining the serious nature of the topic. Finding the right balance requires sensitivity and attention to the overall tone and message of your podcast.

Another area to consider is the use of silence. While it might seem counterintuitive, strategically placed silence can be a powerful tool for emphasis and emotional impact. A brief pause after a powerful statement or a moment of dramatic tension can allow the listener to fully absorb the information and experience the intended emotion. Silence is a powerful tool that often gets overlooked.

Finally, let's not forget the importance of high-quality audio. Using poor-quality music or sound effects can severely detract from the overall listening experience. Invest in good-quality audio files, and make sure they are properly mixed and mastered. This means ensuring your audio levels are balanced, your music and sound effects complement the vocals, and everything is clear and free of distortion.

Regularly review your use of music and sound effects in your podcasts. Listen back to your episodes and critically evaluate whether your choices enhance or detract from the listening experience. Gather feedback from your listeners. Are they enjoying the audio elements, or are they finding them distracting? Use this feedback to inform your future choices and continuously refine your approach to sound design. Remember, the goal is to create a rich and immersive listening experience that keeps your audience engaged and coming back for more. The strategic use of music and sound effects is a significant component of achieving that goal. By mastering this aspect of podcast production, you will elevate your podcast to a higher level of professionalism and engagement

PART IV
DISTRIBUTION

14
GETTING IT OUT THERE

How you decide to disseminate your podcast is as important as the content within it. Ideally, you want to put your show between as many ears as possible.

Podcast distribution is a world that is constantly evolving. While this chapter explores some of the currently popular platforms, new options are emerging every month. Do your own research online before making the distribution decision.

While many options exist, this section focuses on three popular and widely used platforms: Libsyn, Buzzsprout, and Spotify for Creators (formerly Anchor.fm), comparing their features, pricing models, and user-friendliness to help you make an informed decision.

Libsyn has long been a stalwart in the podcast hosting world, known for its reliability and extensive feature set. Its strengths lie in its robust infrastructure, offering high-quality hosting and reliable delivery. Libsyn provides detailed analytics, allowing you to track downloads, listener demographics, and other valuable metrics that inform your podcast strategy. Their advanced features, such as podcasting-specific SEO tools and the ability to create custom RSS feeds, are appealing to those who value control and flexibility. The platform's interface is relatively intuitive, although it might have a steeper learning curve for absolute beginners compared to others.

Libsyn's pricing structure is tiered, with costs increasing based on storage and bandwidth needs. While it's not the cheapest option, the reliability and advanced features often justify the investment, particularly for established podcasts with a large audience. One potential drawback is that the pricing can become substantial for podcasts generating significant traffic, demanding careful consideration of your projected growth.

Buzzsprout offers a compelling alternative, prioritizing ease of use and a streamlined interface. It's an excellent choice for podcasters new to the game, with its simple setup and intuitive dashboard making it easy to navigate even without prior experience.

Buzzsprout boasts automatic distribution to major platforms like Apple Podcasts, Spotify, and Google Podcasts, simplifying the often-complex process of getting your podcast heard. The platform also offers detailed analytics, providing insights into your listener base.

However, the analytics are somewhat less comprehensive than Libsyn's, focusing more on broad trends rather than granular details. Buzzsprout's pricing is also tiered, but generally more affordable than Libsyn at the lower tiers, making it attractive for budget-conscious podcasters. The platform's strengths lie in its simplicity and affordability, making it a popular choice for those who prioritize ease of use without sacrificing features. However, the lack of advanced features, such as custom RSS feeds, might be a limiting factor for podcasts that require greater control over their distribution.

Spotify for Creators (formerly known as Anchor.fm), The platform's interface is free, incredibly user-friendly, simplifying the podcast creation and publishing process. Spotify for Creators does not provide automatic distribution to a range of podcast platforms, but does provide links to other platforms to help you distribute the podcast yourself. It also includes integrated tools for creating and editing your podcast episodes directly within the platform. This all-in-one approach simplifies the workflow considerably.

However, Spotify for Creators comes with limitations. Monetization options are limited, and the analytics provided are less detailed than those offered by Libsyn or Buzzsprout. As your podcast grows, you may outgrow the free plan and find yourself needing the more advanced tools available on paid platforms.

Comparing these three platforms reveals key differences in their approach. Libsyn excels in its reliability, advanced features, and granular analytics, making it suitable for established podcasts with a substantial audience and specific technical needs. Buzzsprout prioritizes user-friendliness and affordability, making it ideal for beginners and those who value a streamlined workflow. Spotify for Creators offers an attractive free entry point, simplifying podcast creation for those seeking a low-barrier-to-entry option. Ultimately, the best platform for you depends on your specific needs, budget, and technical expertise. Consider your current audience size, your future growth projections, your monetization plans, and the level of control you need over your podcast's distribution and analytics.

Beyond these three, numerous other hosting platforms exist, each with its strengths and weaknesses. Some offer specialized features tailored to specific podcasting niches, while others cater to larger enterprise-level productions. Explore these alternatives if the platforms discussed above don't perfectly align with your needs. Other options include Podbean, Spreaker, and Blubrry. Invest some time in comparing their features, pricing, and support to ensure you make the most informed decision. Always check reviews from other podcasters to gain additional perspectives on platform reliability, ease of use, and customer service.

Choosing a platform is only the first step. Understanding the implications of that choice extends to the long-term management of your podcast. This includes regularly reviewing your platform's offerings, adapting to any changes in their pricing structures or features, and remaining aware of any improvements offered by competing platforms. Over time, you may find that a platform that initially met your needs no longer serves you optimally.

TRANSFERRING TO A DIFFERENT PLATFORM

Transferring your podcast to a new hosting platform can be a complex process, requiring careful planning and attention to detail.

Make sure to back up your entire podcast before initiating the transfer, creating a complete archive of all your podcast episodes, show notes, and associated media files Then, carefully examine your chosen new platform's import capabilities. Many platforms provide tools to help simplify the transfer process, however, each platform has its idiosyncrasies so reviewing detailed instructions specific to your target platform and your original platform is critical.

Throughout this process, be prepared for potential issues, such as file incompatibility or errors during the upload. Allow ample time for the transfer process, as it can be time-consuming depending on your podcast's size and the volume of data involved. Make sure to thoroughly test your podcast feed after the transfer, ensuring that all episodes are accessible and playing correctly on various podcasting platforms. Regularly checking your analytics will reveal any anomalies and help ensure a smooth transition for your listeners.

THE TAKE-AWAY

Selecting the right podcast hosting platform is a strategic decision that affects multiple aspects of your podcast's success. This involves careful consideration of your present and future needs, your technical proficiency, and your budget. While Libsyn, Buzzsprout, and Spotify for Creators represent three popular choices, each with its distinct advantages and disadvantages, remember to explore other available options to find the perfect fit for your podcast. And always remember that migrating your podcast to a different platform, though potentially challenging, remains a viable option as your podcast evolves and your needs change. With careful planning and execution, you can ensure a smooth transition without disrupting your audience's access to your content.

15
UNDERSTANDING PODCAST RSS FEEDS AND XML

Having chosen a podcast hosting platform, the next step is understanding how your podcast reaches listeners: through RSS feeds. While you won't typically manually create an RSS feed—your hosting platform handles that—grasping its function can help with troubleshooting and optimizing your podcast's discoverability.

Think of your podcast RSS feed as a digital table of contents, a constantly updated index that tells podcast apps where to find your audio files.

RSS, or Really Simple Syndication (or, more accurately, Rich Site Summary), is a web feed format used to publish frequently updated content, such as podcast episodes. It's an XML (Extensible Markup Language) based file that includes metadata about your podcast, along with a link to each episode's audio file. This metadata includes information like the podcast title, description, author, artwork, episode titles, descriptions, and publication dates. This comprehensive information allows podcast apps to quickly and efficiently access and display your podcast's content. The RSS feed also acts as a dynamic link, automatically updating whenever you upload a new episode.

It's a concise, machine-readable package containing all the information necessary for podcast apps to seamlessly display your podcast to listeners. The accuracy and completeness of these elements directly influence the usability and discoverability of your podcast. Inaccurate or missing information can cause problems with podcast app compatibility, leading to frustration for your listeners.

Imagine a library catalogue. The RSS feed acts as that catalogue, listing all your podcast episodes (books) with their titles, descriptions (summaries), and locations (shelf numbers—the URLs to your audio files). Podcast apps (library patrons) use this catalogue to find and access your episodes. A well-maintained and accurate catalogue ensures smooth access to your content.

Conversely, an incomplete or inaccurate catalogue makes it difficult to locate the material. This analogy highlights the role the RSS feed plays in podcast distribution.

Beyond the basic elements, RSS feeds can include additional elements, often specific to certain podcast directories or platforms.

These extensions can enrich your podcast's metadata, improving its visibility. For instance, itunes:keywords can help categorize your podcast for improved searchability in Apple Podcasts. Similarly, itunes:image specifies the podcast artwork, helpful for visual identification in podcast apps. Many hosting platforms automatically generate these additional elements, optimizing your feed for various directories.

However, understanding the basics of RSS feeds and XML helps you troubleshoot problems. If your podcast isn't appearing correctly on a certain platform, examining the RSS feed can often pinpoint the issue. Errors in the URL, for example, will prevent listeners from accessing your audio files. Similarly, issues with the pubDate can lead to episodes appearing out of order. While you won't typically edit your RSS feed directly, understanding its structure equips you to better communicate with your hosting platform's support team when needed.

It's also important to understand that your podcast hosting platform handles the technical intricacies of generating and maintaining your RSS feed. This means you usually won't interact directly with the XML code. The platform automatically updates the RSS feed every time you upload a new episode, ensuring that your podcast apps always have access to the latest information. This automation simplifies the process significantly, freeing you to concentrate on creating high-quality content.

However, knowing the key components of the RSS feed empowers you to make more informed decisions about your podcast's metadata. While your hosting platform handles the technical generation of the feed, you control the content itself—the title, description, and episode information. The accuracy and completeness of this metadata are critical for your podcast's success. Compelling descriptions and strategically chosen keywords enhance search engine optimization (SEO), improving your podcast's visibility and discoverability.

Validating your RSS feed using online validators is a good practice. These tools check the XML structure for errors, ensuring it conforms to RSS standards. This preventative measure can avoid compatibility problems across different podcast apps, ensuring your podcast is correctly displayed and accessible to a wider audience. Regular validation is particularly important after significant changes to your podcast feed, such as adding new categories or changing episode URLs.

Another important consideration is the interaction between your RSS feed and podcast directories like Apple Podcasts, Spotify, Google Podcasts, and others. When you submit your podcast to these directories, you provide them with the URL of your RSS feed. The directories then use this feed to index your podcast and display its information to their users. The accuracy and quality of your RSS feed directly impact how your podcast is represented within these directories. A poorly structured or inaccurate feed can lead to problems with indexing, resulting in lower discoverability and potentially impacting your listenership.

THE TAKE-AWAY

A well-structured and accurate feed ensures that listeners can easily access your episodes, browse your podcast's archive, and have a seamless listening experience. Conversely, issues with your feed can lead to frustration, missed episodes, or inability to subscribe, potentially driving listeners away. Investing time in understanding the fundamentals of your RSS feed is an investment in your audience's satisfaction and ultimately, your podcast's success. It's a behind-the-scenes element that greatly influences the user experience, highlighting the importance of a functioning and correctly formatted RSS feed.

16
SUBMITTING YOUR PODCAST TO DIRECTORIES

With your podcast hosted and your RSS feed diligently working in the background, the next significant step is distributing your content to the world, if you haven't chosen a platform that will do this automatically.

Podcast directories act as gateways, connecting your carefully crafted content with a vast audience of potential listeners. The most prominent podcast directories include Apple Podcasts (formerly iTunes), Spotify, Google Podcasts, and Stitcher, among others. Each directory has its own submission process and requirements, but the core principles remain consistent: providing accurate and engaging information about your podcast. Think of these directories as highly curated online libraries; the more compelling and well-organized your submission, the more likely your podcast is to be featured prominently, drawing the attention of new listeners.

Before embarking on the submission process, carefully review each directory's guidelines. These guidelines are often detailed and specific, providing information about the required metadata, artwork specifications, and other requirements. Ignoring these guidelines can result in rejection or delays, hindering your podcast's launch. Take the time to understand the specific requirements of each platform, tailoring your submission accordingly.

A common requirement across all directories is high-quality podcast artwork. This is the visual representation of your podcast, often the first impression potential listeners have. A compelling and well-designed image can significantly impact your podcast's appeal and discoverability. Invest in professional artwork design, ensuring it is visually engaging, relevant to your content, and adheres to the size and format specifications outlined by each directory. A blurry or poorly designed image can significantly detract from your podcast's professional image.

Similarly, accurate and compelling descriptions are necessary for search engine optimization (SEO) and for attracting potential listeners. The description should concisely but compellingly summarize your podcast's content, highlighting its unique selling points and target audience. Use clear, concise language, avoiding jargon or overly technical terms unless your target audience is highly specialized. Include relevant keywords that accurately reflect your podcast's content, enhancing its searchability within the directory.

Beyond the basic descriptions, consider additional metadata. Many directories allow for categorizing your podcast with specific genres and keywords. Use these features strategically to increase your podcast's discoverability. Research relevant categories and keywords that accurately represent your podcast's content and target audience. Thorough keyword research will ensure your podcast is easily found when listeners search within the directory.

For example, a podcast about historical events in the American West might include categories such as "History," "American History," "Western History," and keywords such as "Wild West," "Cowboys," "Gold Rush," and specific historical events. The more specific and relevant the keywords, the more likely listeners interested in your topic are to discover your podcast.

Once your podcast artwork, descriptions, and metadata are prepared, the submission process varies slightly depending on the directory. Apple Podcasts, for example, requires you to submit your RSS feed URL directly through their website. Other directories may have slightly different procedures, potentially involving the use of third-party submission services. In all cases, carefully follow the instructions provided by each directory, double-checking all submitted information for accuracy. A minor error can lead to rejection or delays, so pay attention to detail.

During the submission process, you will typically encounter a review period. This period can vary in length, depending on the directory and the volume of submissions. Be patient and allow sufficient time for your podcast to be reviewed and potentially approved. If your submission is rejected, review the feedback provided by the directory, identifying any areas needing improvement. Common reasons for rejection include incomplete or inaccurate metadata, substandard artwork, or violation of the directory's terms of service. Addressing these issues and resubmitting your podcast may be necessary.

While most directories offer straightforward submission processes, you might encounter occasional technical glitches or delays. If your submission encounters problems, consult the directory's help center or support team for assistance. Detailed documentation and contact information are usually provided on their websites. These support resources can provide valuable assistance in resolving any submission-related issues.

Submitting your podcast to multiple directories expands your potential reach. Consider prioritizing the directories that best align with your target audience and podcast content. For instance, if you cater to a younger demographic, prioritizing Spotify and YouTube might be beneficial. If you have a niche topic, focusing on less mainstream directories with a dedicated audience might be a more effective strategy. A strategic approach to directory selection can significantly enhance your podcast's visibility and attract a relevant audience.

Real-world examples highlight the importance of careful preparation and submission. A podcast with well-crafted artwork, thorough descriptions, and strategically chosen keywords is more likely to attract listeners. On the other hand, a podcast with a poorly designed image or a vague description is less likely to be discovered and subscribed to. Observing successful podcasts and analyzing their submission approaches can provide invaluable insights into effective strategies.

Remember that submitting your podcast to directories is an ongoing process. Regularly monitor your podcast's performance within each directory, tracking metrics like downloads, subscriptions, and listener feedback. This data provides important insights into your podcast's audience engagement and helps you adapt your strategy.

For example, if a particular directory yields low engagement, you might need to re-evaluate your metadata or artwork, or even consider targeting a different audience.

THE TAKE-AWAY

Distributing your podcast through major directories is a vital component of your overall podcasting strategy. It's more than just a technical process; it's about presenting your podcast in the most compelling and accessible way to a global audience. By carefully preparing your submission, rigorously following each directory's guidelines, and actively monitoring your podcast's performance, you can significantly increase your chances of success, growing your audience, and reaching a wider listener base. It is a continuous optimization process, constantly refining your approach based on data and feedback.

PART V
SELLING IT

17
PODCAST MARKETING AND PROMOTION STRATEGIES

SOCIAL MEDIA: BUILDING COMMUNITY

Social media platforms have become indispensable tools for podcast promotion. They offer a direct line of communication with potential listeners, allowing you to build a community around your show and engage with your audience on a personal level. However, a haphazard approach won't cut it. Strategic planning is vital.

First, identify the platforms best suited to your target audience. A younger demographic might be more active on TikTok and Instagram, while a more mature audience might favor Facebook or Twitter/BlueSky. Don't spread yourself too thin; focus your efforts on the platforms where your ideal listeners are most likely to congregate.

Once you've chosen your platforms, craft a compelling social media presence. This starts with creating engaging profiles that accurately reflect your podcast's brand and tone. Use high-quality visuals, including your podcast artwork, and write concise, informative bios that capture the essence of your show. Think of your social media profiles as virtual storefronts for your podcast. They are the first impression many potential listeners will have, so make them count.

Beyond static profiles, you need consistent and engaging content. Don't just post episode announcements; offer valuable content that resonates with your target audience. This might include behind-the-scenes glimpses of your podcasting process, snippets of upcoming episodes, polls related to your show's topics, or even interactive Q&A sessions. The goal is to provide value beyond just promoting your episodes.

Consider using different content formats. Short video clips, visually engaging infographics, or even short audio clips from your podcast can increase engagement and reach a wider audience. Remember, people consume content differently on various platforms. Adapt your content accordingly to resonate with the platform's characteristics.

Engage actively with your followers. Respond to comments, participate in relevant conversations, and foster a sense of community. This two-way interaction builds loyalty and transforms your social media presence from a one-way broadcast into a vibrant hub of interaction and discussion. Consider running contests or giveaways to increased engagement and grow your following organically.

Analyze your social media analytics regularly. Most platforms offer detailed insights into post performance, follower demographics, and audience engagement. Use this data to refine your strategy, optimizing your posting schedule, content formats, and overall approach. What content performs best? What times of day are your followers most active? Continuously analyzing these metrics allows for a data-driven approach to social media marketing.

EMAIL MARKETING: NURTURING YOUR LOYAL LISTENERS

While social media is excellent for building a broad audience, email marketing offers a more direct and personal approach to reaching your most dedicated listeners.

Start by creating a compelling opt-in form on your podcast's website. This form should clearly explain the benefits of subscribing to your email list, such as receiving exclusive content, early access to new episodes, or invitations to special events. Incentivize sign-ups with a free lead magnet, such as a downloadable resource or a bonus episode, to encourage potential listeners to join your email list.

Create a series of emails that deliver value to your subscribers. Don't just bombard them with episode announcements; offer valuable content, such as blog posts, articles, or even short audio clips related to your podcast's theme. Segment your email list based on listener preferences or demographics if possible to send more targeted and relevant content.

Email marketing automation tools can streamline your efforts. These tools can automate email delivery, personalize messages based on listener data, and track the effectiveness of your campaigns. This automation can save you a significant amount of time and effort.

Regularly analyze your email analytics to track open rates, click-through rates, and unsubscribe rates. Use this data to optimize your email content and delivery schedule. What types of emails resonate most with your subscribers? What days and times are the best for sending emails? Continuously refine your strategy based on the data you collect.

CROSS-PROMOTION: EXPANDING YOUR REACH THROUGH COLLABORATION

Cross-promotion, collaborating with other podcasters in your niche, can be highly effective for expanding your audience and increasing your podcast's visibility. Find podcasts with a similar target audience and complementary content. Consider guest appearances, joint episodes, or even sponsored segments to reach new listeners through an established audience.

When collaborating with other podcasters, ensure that the collaboration feels authentic and beneficial to both parties. Avoid forced or unnatural partnerships. A genuine connection between the podcasts will lead to a more successful collaboration and enhanced audience appeal.

TRACKING KEY PERFORMANCE INDICATORS (KPIS): MEASURING YOUR SUCCESS

Marketing efforts require data-driven analysis. Tracking Key Performance Indicators (KPIs) helps assess the effectiveness of your podcast's marketing strategy. These KPIs should be relevant to your marketing goals and should track your progress towards achieving those goals.

Key metrics to monitor include:

Download numbers: The number of downloads per episode and overall. This indicates the reach of your podcast.

Subscriber growth: The rate at which new subscribers are added to your podcast feed. A healthy growth rate is an important indicator of success.

Website traffic: Track the number of visitors to your podcast's website, indicating listener engagement.

Social media engagement: Monitor metrics such as likes, comments, shares, and retweets to gauge audience interaction.

Email open and click-through rates: Measure the effectiveness of your email marketing campaigns.

Analyzing your KPIs regularly and adapting your strategy based on the insights gained a habit shared by best-in-class podcasters. By implementing these marketing strategies, constantly monitoring your KPIs, and refining your approach based on data, you can significantly increase your podcast's reach, build a loyal listenership, and achieve your podcasting goals. Remember, podcast marketing is an ongoing process requiring consistent effort and adaptation.

18
ANALYZING PODCAST PERFORMANCE AND METRICS

Analyzing podcast performance isn't just about vanity metrics; it's about understanding your audience, refining your content, and maximizing your reach. While creating compelling audio is obviously important, a blind approach to production without understanding how your podcast performs is like sailing without a compass. Data-driven decision making is necessary for sustainable podcast growth.

This section delves into metrics, the tools to track them, and how to translate raw numbers into actionable strategies.

Your podcast hosting platform is your primary source of performance data. Most platforms – whether it's Libsyn, Buzzsprout, Spotify for Creators or something other – provide comprehensive dashboards displaying key performance indicators (KPIs). Familiarize yourself with the specifics of your chosen platform's analytics. While the exact metrics and presentation might differ slightly, the core data points remain consistent across providers. Understanding these dashboards is fundamental to effectively managing and improving your podcast's success.

One of the most fundamental metrics is **downloads**. This

simple number represents the total number of times your episodes have been downloaded. While seemingly straightforward, downloads can reveal a great deal. A sudden spike could indicate successful marketing campaign or a particularly engaging episode. Conversely, a consistent decline might warrant a review of your content strategy or marketing efforts. Pay attention not only to overall download numbers, but also to individual episode performance. Which episodes resonate most with your audience? Why? This granular level of analysis can inform future content creation.

Beyond raw download counts, many platforms offer data on **listens or plays** . This metric distinguishes between a download and actual listening time. A high download count but low listening time suggests a potential problem with your content's engagement. Listeners may be downloading but not completing the episode. This information suggests the need to address aspects like pacing, audio quality, or content relevance. Are your introductions too long? Is the flow disjointed? Careful analysis can pinpoint areas for improvement.

Unique downloads distinguish between repeat downloads by the same listener and a new listener engaging with your content. This metric offers a more accurate representation of your podcast's reach. If you're seeing high repeat downloads but low unique downloads, this suggests a loyal listener base but limited audience growth. This indicates a need to focus on expanding your marketing efforts to attract new listeners.

Audience demographics provide valuable insights into your listeners. Many hosting platforms provide data on listener location, age range, and device usage. This information can be invaluable for refining your targeting strategies in future marketing campaigns. If you find that a large portion of your audience is located in a specific geographic area, you can tailor your promotion efforts to that region, or possibly even create content relevant to their interests or culture. Similarly, understanding the age range of your audience helps tailor your content and marketing approach.

Average listening time is a critical metric indicative of listener engagement. This metric reveals how much of each episode your listeners are consuming. Many viewers have short attention spans, and it's generally a good idea to keep podcasts short. Low average listening times suggest problems with the content's length, engagement, or overall appeal. Are you losing listeners in the middle of your episodes? This metric allows you to analyze where in your episode you are losing listener engagement, pointing to areas for improvement in pacing, content or production quality.

Audience retention is closely tied to average listening time. It goes a step further by showing how listeners progress through each episode. A steep drop-off in listeners early in the episode points to a problem with your introduction or opening segment. A consistent decline throughout the episode may suggest the overall content isn't holding interest. Analyzing the retention graph allows for a deep dive into listener behavior.

Your hosting platform's analytics also provide valuable information on **subscriber growth** . Are you gaining new subscribers? What's the rate of growth? This is a direct reflection of your podcast's overall appeal and the success of your marketing initiatives. Slow growth could mean your marketing efforts need refinement.

Beyond the metrics provided directly by your hosting platform, consider integrating other analytics tools. For instance, if you have a website associated with your podcast, analyze website traffic and user behavior using tools like Google Analytics. This provides a broader perspective on your overall audience engagement. Website traffic patterns can reveal what content is most engaging on your website, which can inform future podcast episode topics. Cross-referencing your website analytics with your podcast hosting platform data can provide a holistic view of your listener's engagement.

But numbers alone don't tell the whole story. You must actively interpret the data and use it to make informed decisions. For example, if you see a consistent drop-off in listening time at a particular point in your episodes, you might consider re-evaluating that segment of your show. Is the content too dense? Is the pacing too slow? Is the audio quality subpar? The data provides the clues; your expertise provides the solutions.

Let's consider a hypothetical example. Imagine a podcast focusing on personal finance. Analyzing the data reveals that episodes focusing on investment strategies have high download and listening numbers, while episodes on budgeting receive fewer listens and lower average listening time. This suggests a mismatch between listener interest and content. The podcast creator might then adjust future content, focusing on more investment-related topics, or revising the budgeting episodes to be more engaging and accessible. Perhaps incorporating interviews with financial experts or using case studies would make the content more appealing.

Another example: Let's say a podcast about historical events notices a sudden surge in downloads for a specific episode. Analyzing the platform's data might show that the increase in downloads originated from a specific social media campaign. This would validate that marketing effort and encourage similar strategies in the future. Alternatively, a low download number for a particular episode might warrant revisiting the episode's title and description for better searchability and more compelling wording.

THE TAKE-AWAY

Data analysis is an ongoing process, not a one-time event. Regularly review your analytics, at least monthly, to track your progress, identify trends, and make necessary adjustments. Don't be afraid to experiment with different content formats, episode lengths, and marketing strategies. Use the data to guide your experiments and measure their effectiveness. Remember, the goal is not just to produce a podcast but to cultivate a thriving community of engaged listeners.

Understanding and using your data is the key to unlocking that potential.

19

WORKING WITH SPONSORS AND OTHER MONETIZATION STRATEGIES

Let's talk about monetization. This isn't about chasing quick riches; it's about creating a financially viable model that allows you to continue creating the content your audience loves—and get paid for it.

SPONSORSHIP

One of the most prevalent methods is sponsorship. Finding the right sponsors requires a strategic approach. First, you need to define your target audience. Who are your listeners? What are their interests, demographics, and purchasing habits? This understanding of your audience will allow you to identify sponsors whose products or services align with their needs and preferences.

A mismatch between your listeners and a sponsor can lead to a disengaged audience and an ineffective campaign for the sponsor. Authenticity is key here; forcing a sponsorship that doesn't resonate with your audience will damage your credibility.

Once you've identified your ideal sponsor profile, you can begin the search. Start by reaching out to companies whose products or services are relevant to your podcast's content and audience. Your podcast analytics will be invaluable here; look at the demographic data to target companies that are a good fit. You can also access online platforms and directories specifically designed to connect podcasters with sponsors. These platforms typically allow you to create a profile outlining your podcast's reach, audience demographics, and engagement metrics. This provides potential sponsors with the information they need to assess the value proposition.

Negotiating sponsorship deals requires clear communication and a strong understanding of your podcast's value. You need to quantify your audience reach and engagement rates. This involves presenting data such as download numbers, listener demographics, and website traffic. You'll also need to establish clear expectations concerning the type of advertising you're comfortable with, the frequency of mentions, and the duration of the sponsorship. Develop a media kit outlining these details. This kit should include your podcast's description, target audience demographics, listenership statistics, and examples of previous successful campaigns (if applicable). Maintain a professional demeanor in all communication; this builds trust and encourages long-term partnerships.

Beyond simple audio advertisements, consider innovative ways to integrate your sponsors. This could involve creating a sponsored segment, co-hosting an episode, or developing a series of short branded videos accompanying episodes. The more creative you are, the more engaging you make the integration. But always prioritize the listening experience. Avoid aggressive or jarring advertising. The goal is seamless integration, not a disruptive interruption to the flow of your content. A well-integrated sponsorship becomes part of the story, not an intrusive advertisement. Think of it as creating a valuable collaboration rather than a purely transactional relationship. Mutual benefit should always be the guiding principle.

Ethical considerations are vital. Always disclose any sponsorships transparently. Never endorse a product or service you don't genuinely believe in. Your credibility is your most valuable asset.

Consumers are becoming increasingly savvy and can easily spot inauthentic endorsements. Transparency builds trust. If you're unsure about a sponsorship opportunity, it's always better to err on the side of caution and decline it.

Let's consider some real-world examples. A podcast about sustainable living might partner with an eco-friendly clothing company, naturally weaving the brand into discussions about ethical fashion. A true crime podcast might collaborate with a genealogy service, helping listeners uncover family history relevant to the cases discussed. A food podcast might work with local restaurants, offering listeners discounts or promoting special events.

The key is to find natural synergies that benefit both the podcast and the sponsor.

AFFILIATE MARKETING

However, sponsorship isn't the only avenue for podcast monetization. Affiliate marketing presents another viable strategy. This involves promoting other companies' products or services and earning a commission on each sale generated through your custom affiliate link. Choose products and services that genuinely align with your podcast's themes and audience, maintaining that all-important authenticity. Don't simply fill your episodes with affiliate links; it feels spammy. Instead, subtly incorporate them into relevant conversations.

MERCH AND CROWDFUNDING

Selling merchandise is yet another option. This might involve creating branded merchandise like t-shirts, mugs, or hats. You could also offer downloadable content like bonus episodes or exclusive interviews.

Exploring options like crowdfunding platforms can also be helpful. These platforms allow listeners to directly support the creation of your content through voluntary donations.

Alternately, you might consider offering premium content or exclusive access to certain episodes or features for a recurring subscription fee. This might include bonus episodes, early access to new content, ad-free listening, or access to a private community forum.

For smaller podcasts that may not have the extensive reach to attract major sponsors, these alternative methods can be particularly valuable. They offer avenues for monetization that don't rely on attracting large-scale sponsorships.

Building a strong community and engaging with your listeners regularly is necessary for the success of such endeavors. Transparency is paramount; keep your listeners informed about your progress and how their contributions are being utilized.

Building a strong, engaged audience is the foundation of any successful monetization strategy. Focus on creating high-quality content that resonates with your listeners, fostering a community around your podcast, and interacting with your audience. This will make your podcast more attractive to sponsors and will increase the likelihood of success with alternative monetization methods.

Remember, your podcast is a business. While creating compelling content is your core function, understanding and implementing a suitable monetization strategy is vital for its long-term viability. Don't be afraid to experiment with different approaches and adapt your strategies based on what works best for your specific podcast and audience. Continuously analyzing your performance data will help you identify what resonates and make informed decisions about your future monetization efforts. Success in podcasting often comes down to a blend of creative storytelling and savvy business sense. Mastering both will lead to a thriving and enduring podcast.

20
CREATING A PODCAST WEBSITE AND ONLINE PRESENCE

Building a strong online presence contributes to a podcast's success as its audio quality and content. Your podcast website serves as your central hub, a digital home where listeners can easily access your episodes, learn about you, and connect with your community. Creating a professional-looking and user-friendly website is an investment that pays dividends in listener engagement and overall podcast growth.

The first step is choosing a suitable website platform. Several options cater specifically to podcasters, offering streamlined interfaces and features designed to simplify the process. Popular choices include WordPress (with podcasting plugins), Squarespace, and Wix. Each platform offers varying levels of customization and requires different levels of technical expertise. WordPress, while offering the greatest flexibility, demands a more hands-on approach and might require some familiarity with web design principles or the use of plugins.

Squarespace and Wix, on the other hand, provide user-friendly drag-and-drop interfaces, making them ideal for those with limited technical skills. Consider your technical proficiency and design preferences when making your decision.

Regardless of your chosen platform, several key elements should be included on your podcast website. A prominent section featuring your latest episodes is a must, with clear titles, descriptions, and easily accessible download or streaming links. Integrate your podcast feed (usually an RSS feed) seamlessly, ensuring that listeners can effortlessly subscribe through their preferred podcast apps. Include high-quality images or artwork representing your podcast brand. Consistency in visuals enhances the professional appearance of your site.

Your "About" page should provide a compelling introduction to your podcast, detailing its mission, target audience, and your personal background and motivations. This is where you establish a connection with your listeners on a more personal level. The more relatable and authentic you are, the stronger the connection you'll build. Consider including a brief biography or a captivating story explaining your journey into podcasting.

A contact page makes it easy for listeners to reach you with questions, comments, or feedback. Providing multiple contact options, such as an email address and a contact form, ensures greater accessibility. It's also a good idea to integrate your social media links prominently on your website, encouraging listeners to engage with you on other platforms.

Search Engine Optimization (SEO) is vital for improving your website's visibility in search results. This involves using relevant keywords throughout your website's content, optimizing your images with descriptive alt text, and creating high-quality content that attracts organic traffic. Tools like Google Search Console and SEMrush can help you analyze your website's performance and identify areas for improvement. Don't underestimate the power of compelling titles and meta descriptions for your web pages; they're often the first impression potential listeners have of your podcast.

Building an online community around your podcast fosters

engagement and loyalty. Your website is a prime location for nurturing community interaction. Consider incorporating features like a comment section on your blog posts or episode pages, encouraging listeners to share their thoughts and opinions. Running contests or giveaways can also enhance audience participation and boost website traffic.

Analyzing your website's analytics is necessary for gauging the success of your online presence. Tools like Google Analytics provide valuable insights into your website's traffic, audience demographics, and engagement metrics. By closely monitoring your analytics, you can adapt your content strategy, improve your SEO efforts, and refine your online community-building activities. Pay close attention to bounce rates and time spent on pages. High bounce rates might indicate issues with website navigation or content relevance. Longer time spent on specific pages might highlight particularly engaging content or aspects of your website design.

Beyond your core website, consider the possibility of creating a dedicated email list. This allows you to directly communicate with your most engaged listeners, providing exclusive content and fostering a more personal connection. Regular newsletters with updates on new episodes, bonus content, and community events can build anticipation and loyalty.

In addition to email, consider the benefits of utilizing a podcast hosting platform. These platforms provide more than just a place to store your audio files. Many hosting services offer features like detailed analytics, website integration capabilities, and even monetization tools. They can streamline many of the technical aspects of podcast publishing, allowing you to focus more on content creation and audience engagement.

Creating a successful podcast website and overall online presence requires a strategic, multi-faceted approach. It's not just about creating a website; it's about crafting a digital experience that resonates with your listeners and actively fosters a vibrant community around your podcast. This requires consistent effort, careful planning, and ongoing analysis of your performance data. But the rewards of building a strong online presence are substantial, leading to increased listener engagement, expanded reach, and ultimately, a more successful and sustainable podcast. Regularly reviewing and updating your website and social media strategies will ensure you remain relevant and connected to your audience.

The Take-Away: Your online presence reflects your brand. A cohesive, professional, and engaging online experience will set your podcast apart. Don't view your website and social media simply as promotional tools; rather, consider them extensions of your podcast, enriching the listener experience and building a loyal community. Invest the time and effort to create a compelling digital home for your podcast, and you'll see a tangible return in the form of increased listener engagement and a more vibrant community.

21
COLLABORATING AND BUILDING A NETWORK

Collaborating with other podcasters is not merely a strategic move; it's a cornerstone of sustainable growth in the podcasting landscape. The podcasting community thrives on mutual support and shared success. Building a strong network of fellow creators isn't just about boosting your listener numbers; it's about enriching your own podcasting journey through shared experiences, knowledge exchange, and the creation of synergistic opportunities.

One of the most effective ways to find potential collaborators is to actively engage within the podcasting community. Attend industry events, both online and offline. Conferences, workshops, and meetups offer invaluable opportunities to connect with other podcasters, learn from their experiences, and identify potential partners. Online forums and groups dedicated to podcasting provide another avenue for networking. Participate in discussions, share your insights, and actively listen to what others have to say. These virtual spaces are teeming with potential collaborators who share your passions and may have complementary audiences.

Identifying potential collaborators requires a strategic approach.

Start by analyzing your podcast's target audience. Who are your listeners? What are their interests, demographics, and consumption habits? Understanding your audience will help you identify podcasters who cater to similar demographics or whose content aligns with your own. For example, if your podcast focuses on sustainable living, collaborating with a podcast about gardening or vegan cooking could be highly beneficial, as their listeners likely share similar values and interests. This alignment ensures that your cross-promotional efforts reach a receptive audience.

Don't limit your search to podcasters in the exact same niche.

Consider collaborating with podcasts that complement your content, even if they don't directly overlap. A podcast about personal finance could find a strong synergy with a podcast about entrepreneurship, as both target audiences share an interest in improving their financial well-being. Similarly, a history podcast might benefit from collaborating with a podcast focused on historical fiction, leveraging each other's distinct strengths to reach a broader audience. The key is to find connections that resonate with your listeners and offer mutual benefits.

Reaching out to other podcasters requires a professional and respectful approach. Before initiating contact, do your research.

Listen to a few episodes of the podcast you're interested in collaborating with, to ensure alignment with your values and podcast style. Familiarize yourself with their work, their audience, and their overall brand. Your initial outreach should be genuine and well-considered, not a generic template.

Craft a personalized email or message explaining your podcast and why you believe a collaboration would be mutually beneficial. Highlight the shared audience interests and the potential synergistic opportunities. Suggest specific collaboration ideas, such as guest appearances, cross-promotion of episodes, or joint social media campaigns. Be mindful of the other podcaster's time and avoid overwhelming them with lengthy requests. Keep your initial contact brief, professional, and focused on the value you can offer. A concise and compelling proposition is much more effective than a lengthy, rambling message.

Consider different types of collaborations. Guest appearances are a classic and highly effective strategy. Appearing on another podcast exposes your podcast to a new audience, while also providing valuable content for your collaborator. Reciprocity is key; offer to have them on your podcast as well. This creates a mutually beneficial arrangement, strengthening the relationship and maximizing the reach of both podcasts.

Cross-promotion of episodes is another powerful tactic. Announce each other's episodes on your respective podcasts, directing your listeners to check out your collaborator's work. This can be done through verbal mentions, show notes, or even dedicated segments.

Joint social media campaigns can amplify the reach of both podcasts. Collaborate on social media posts, creating shared content that promotes both podcasts to a wider audience. The key is to create compelling and engaging content that resonates with your combined audience.

Building a successful collaboration hinges on clear communication and mutual respect. Discuss your goals, expectations, and timelines upfront to avoid misunderstandings. Establish a collaborative workflow that works for both parties, ensuring that the process is efficient and enjoyable. Regular communication is vital throughout the collaboration to track progress, address any challenges, and maintain a positive working relationship.

Remember that networking extends beyond formal collaborations.

Building relationships within the podcasting community is an ongoing process. Engage with other podcasters' content, offer supportive comments and feedback, and participate in industry conversations. By actively engaging with your peers, you build trust and establish connections that can lead to future collaborations and mutual support. Consider creating a mentorship relationship with a more experienced podcaster. Their guidance can be invaluable in navigating the challenges of podcasting and developing your skills.

THE TAKE-AWAY

The podcasting world is a vibrant and supportive community. Building a strong network of collaborators and fellow creators isn't just about self-promotion; it's about fostering a collaborative environment where everyone benefits. By actively engaging with the community, identifying potential partners strategically, and approaching collaborations with professionalism and respect, you can leverage the power of networking to propel your podcast to new heights. The success of your podcast is intrinsically linked to the success of the broader podcasting ecosystem; collaborative efforts amplify the impact of each individual podcast and contribute to the overall growth of the industry. This collaborative spirit is vital in the ever-evolving world of podcasting. The benefits of fostering a supportive network extend far beyond immediate cross-promotional gains; they establish a foundation for sustainable growth, shared learning, and mutual success in the long run.

22

STAYING CURRENT WITH PODCASTING TRENDS AND TECHNOLOGIES

The dynamic nature of podcasting demands continuous learning and adaptation. Staying ahead of the curve requires more than just passion; it necessitates a commitment to ongoing professional development. The podcasting landscape is constantly evolving, with new technologies, platforms, and listener preferences emerging regularly. Failing to adapt to these changes can leave your podcast lagging behind, losing its competitive edge and potentially its audience.

One of the most effective strategies for staying current is to cultivate a habit of continuous learning. This isn't about passively absorbing information; it's about actively seeking out new knowledge and applying it to your podcasting workflow. Subscribe to industry newsletters and podcasts that cover the latest trends and technologies. Many reputable publications and websites offer insightful commentary and analysis on the podcasting industry. These resources often provide early warnings of emerging trends, allowing you to prepare for changes and integrate them into your strategy proactively.

Beyond passively consuming information, actively engage with the podcasting community. Participate in online forums, join relevant social media groups, and network with other podcasters. These platforms offer a wealth of collective knowledge, facilitating the sharing of experiences and best practices. Engage in discussions, ask questions, and offer your insights. This interactive learning environment can significantly enhance your understanding of the industry's dynamics.

Industry conferences and workshops provide invaluable opportunities for professional development. These events bring together podcasters, industry experts, and technology providers, creating a fertile ground for learning and networking. Attending these events allows you to learn firsthand about the latest advancements in podcasting technology and hear directly from successful podcasters about their strategies and experiences. Don't underestimate the power of in-person networking; these connections can lead to invaluable collaborations and mentorship opportunities.

Evaluating new technologies requires a methodical approach. Don't blindly adopt every new tool or platform that appears. Instead, carefully assess the potential benefits and drawbacks of each technology in relation to your specific podcasting needs and resources. Consider factors such as ease of use, cost, compatibility with your existing equipment, and the potential impact on your workflow and audience reach. Start with a thorough research phase. Explore online reviews, compare features and pricing, and look for case studies demonstrating the effectiveness of the technology in real-world podcasting scenarios.

One important area to monitor is audio editing software.

The advancements in AI-powered audio editing tools are transforming the landscape of post-production. Explore the capabilities of various software options, paying attention to features such as noise reduction, audio enhancement, transcription services, and automated mixing capabilities. These tools can significantly improve the quality of your audio and streamline your workflow.

Consider experimenting with free trials or demo versions to test different software options before committing to a purchase.

Another rapidly evolving area is podcast distribution platforms.

Beyond the established giants like Apple Podcasts, Spotify, and Google Podcasts, new platforms are constantly emerging. Each platform has its own strengths and weaknesses in terms of audience reach, analytics capabilities, and monetization options. Staying informed about these changes requires active monitoring of the competitive landscape. Research the characteristics of each platform and consider which ones are most relevant to your target audience and podcasting goals. Diversifying your distribution strategy across multiple platforms can maximize your reach and resilience against changes in the industry.

The technology surrounding podcast hosting is also undergoing continuous evolution. Assess the strengths and limitations of different hosting services, paying close attention to storage capacity, bandwidth limitations, analytics capabilities, and customer support. Choosing a robust and reliable hosting provider ensures that your podcast is consistently available to your listeners. Explore the options offered by various hosting services and select one that best aligns with your needs and budget.

The world of podcast microphones is also constantly expanding, with new models and technologies being released regularly. Evaluate the available options, considering factors such as sound quality, price, versatility, and ease of use. Research different microphone types, including dynamic, condenser, and USB microphones, and select the one that best suits your recording environment and podcast style. Investing in high-quality audio equipment will allow you to deliver a professional and engaging listening experience.

The rise of AI is significantly impacting podcasting, offering both opportunities and challenges. AI-powered tools are now available for transcription, editing, and even generating podcast content. While these tools offer the potential to improve efficiency and productivity, they also raise important considerations about authenticity and creative control. Explore the capabilities of these tools and assess their suitability for your podcasting workflow. Consider the ethical implications of using AI for content creation and ensure that you are using these tools in a responsible and transparent manner.

Adapting to evolving listener preferences is another important factor. Monitor listener feedback, review comments and ratings, and analyze listener demographics to understand their evolving interests and expectations. Use this data to inform your podcast strategy, adjusting your content and format to meet the changing demands of your audience. Conduct regular surveys or polls to gather direct feedback from your listeners and gauge their satisfaction with your podcast. Staying in tune with your audience's preferences will ensure that your podcast remains relevant and engaging.

The use of social media for podcast promotion is another dynamic area requiring continuous attention. Explore the features and functionalities of different social media platforms, experimenting with different content formats and strategies to maximize your reach and engagement. Adapt your social media strategy based on analytics data, continually refining your approach to optimize your podcast's visibility. Monitor emerging social media trends and adapt your strategy to leverage the latest features and functionalities.

THE TAKE-AWAY

Continuously refine your podcasting skills through ongoing education. Explore online courses, workshops, and mentorship opportunities to enhance your knowledge and expertise in podcasting. Consider seeking feedback from experienced podcasters to gain valuable insights and improve your skills. Professional development is not a one-time event; it's an ongoing process that requires continuous effort and commitment. Staying current in the podcasting world is a journey, not a destination. Embrace the continuous learning and adaptation needed to thrive in this ever-changing landscape. The key is to remain proactive, curious, and adaptable, always seeking new ways to enhance your podcast and connect with your audience.

PART VI
RECOMMENDATIONS AND RESOURCES

23
RECOMMENDATIONS

RECOMMENDED EQUIPMENT AND SOFTWARE LIST

Choosing the right equipment and software is essential for producing a high-quality podcast. The market offers a wide range of options, catering to various budgets and needs. I've discussed some of these in previous sections, but am repeating the info again to provide you an easy to access resource list. This section provides a curated list of recommended equipment and software, categorized for clarity and ease of selection. Remember that the "best" setup depends heavily on your specific podcasting style, budget, and technical expertise. Don't feel pressured to purchase everything at once; start with the basics and gradually upgrade as your podcast evolves and your needs change.

MICROPHONES:

For beginners on a tight budget, a USB microphone offers a simple and convenient entry point. The **Yeti** is a popular choice, and features a simple plug-and-play USB interface and a built-in headphone jack to offset the delay or latency often present in analog to digital audio conversations. It features adjustable audio patterns including a cardioid polar pattern effectively minimizes background noise, delivering clear audio in less-than-ideal recording environments. While not as high-end as more expensive options, the Yeti delivers respectable sound quality for its price point. Many positive user reviews highlight its ease of use and reliable performance. You can find comprehensive reviews and purchase options on sites like Amazon and Sweetwater Sound.

Stepping up in quality and price, the **Audio-Technica ATR2100x-USB** is another excellent USB microphone option offering improved clarity and detail. Its rugged construction and versatile mounting options make it suitable for various recording environments. This microphone is widely praised for its ability to handle a wide range of sound sources, making it suitable for both solo podcasts and interviews with multiple guests. Its cardioid polar pattern effectively reduces ambient noise, resulting in cleaner recordings.

For more experienced podcasters or those aiming for professional-grade audio, a condenser microphone paired with an audio interface provides superior sound quality. The **Rode NT1-A** is a highly regarded large-diaphragm condenser microphone known for its exceptionally smooth and detailed sound. It requires an audio interface, adding to the overall cost, but the significant improvement in audio quality justifies the investment for many podcasters. The versatility of this microphone makes it suitable for various applications, from solo voiceovers to musical instrument recording. To use this microphone effectively, you'll need an audio interface, which we will discuss shortly.

Beyond the microphone itself, investing in a good quality microphone shock mount protects ears from unwanted noises, especially for condenser microphones. A shock mount minimizes handling noise and vibrations, preventing unwanted sounds from being picked up by your microphone. The **Rode PSA1** is a popular and affordable shock mount compatible with a wide range of microphones, including the Rode NT1-A.

AUDIO INTERFACES

An audio interface sits between your microphone and your computer, improving the audio signal quality significantly. For beginners venturing beyond a basic USB microphone, the **Focusrite Scarlett Solo** is a reliable and affordable interface. It features a single XLR input, suitable for a single microphone setup, and provides clear, high-quality audio conversion. It's known for its simplicity and ease of use, making it an ideal choice for novice users.

For those needing more inputs, the **Focusrite Scarlett 2i2** offers two XLR inputs, ideal for podcasting interviews or recording multiple audio sources simultaneously. This interface provides more flexibility than the Solo and enables more complex recording scenarios, making it a worthy upgrade as your podcasting needs grow.

HEADPHONES

Closed-back headphones provide the best solution for monitoring your audio during recording to avoid audio bleed (the microphone picking up the sound from your headphones). As mentioned earlier, my trusty **Sony MDR-7506** are a widely acclaimed choice, praised for their comfortable design, accurate sound reproduction, and effective noise isolation. These headphones provide a balanced frequency response, which allows for accurate monitoring of your audio levels and sound quality.

POP FILTERS AND WIND SCREENS

These accessories are vital for minimizing plosives (harsh sounds caused by the "p" and "b" sounds) and wind noise, respectively. A simple pop filter, like those readily available on Amazon, and a foam windscreen are generally sufficient for most podcasting needs. These simple and relatively inexpensive items significantly enhance audio quality by reducing those unwanted bursts and background noises.

SOFTWARE

For audio editing, **Audacity** offers a powerful, free, and open-source option. Its intuitive interface and wide range of features make it suitable for beginners and experienced editors alike. While it lacks some of the advanced features of professional-grade software, Audacity provides all the basic tools needed for editing podcasts. Extensive online resources and tutorials are readily available to assist in learning its capabilities.

Adobe Audition offers a more comprehensive and powerful solution, suitable for more demanding editing tasks and audio enhancements. Its advanced features, such as noise reduction and restoration tools, can greatly improve the quality of your audio. While it comes at a subscription cost, the enhanced capabilities often justify the price for serious podcasters.

GarageBand (Mac) and **Reaper** are also popular choices, each providing various features and capabilities. GarageBand, included with macOS, offers a user-friendly interface and basic audio editing tools, suitable for beginners. Reaper, while having a steeper learning curve, provides unmatched flexibility and features that rival expensive DAWs, often preferred by those willing to invest time in learning a sophisticated audio editor.

PODCAST HOSTING

Several platforms offer podcast hosting services, providing storage, distribution, and analytics. **Libsyn**, **Buzzsprout, and Spotify for Creators** are popular choices, each offering various features and pricing plans. Consider factors such as storage space, bandwidth, analytics capabilities, and customer support when choosing a host.

Your selection should align with your podcast's needs and your budget.

BEYOND THE BASICS

This list focuses on the required equipment and software. As your podcast grows, you might consider investing in further upgrades.

This could include microphones with superior specifications, additional audio interfaces for expanded recording setups, high-quality headphones for more critical listening, and more advanced audio editing software with noise reduction and other specialized tools. Always prioritize improvements that address your specific needs and challenges. Researching reviews and comparing features will always be an important process as you develop your podcast and identify your priorities. Remember that podcasting is an ongoing journey, and your equipment and workflow will evolve along with it. Don't feel the need to buy everything at once—start with the fundamentals and gradually add to your setup as your needs and budget allow.

24
USEFUL WEBSITES AND ONLINE COMMUNITIES

Continuous learning is a part of every success formula. Here is a comprehensive guide to online resources and communities that can significantly enhance your podcasting journey. This curated list of websites and online communities offers a wealth of information, support, and opportunities for connection with fellow podcasters.

Let's start with websites offering tutorials and educational materials. **PodcastMotor** is an excellent starting point for beginners. They offer a wealth of free articles, guides, and video tutorials covering everything from microphone selection and audio editing to podcast promotion and monetization. Their content is well-structured, easy to follow, and regularly updated, making it an invaluable resource for anyone embarking on their podcasting adventure. They also offer paid courses for those seeking more in-depth knowledge. Be sure to explore their blog section for insightful articles on industry trends and best practices.

Another highly recommended website is **Blubrry** . While primarily known for its podcast hosting services, Blubrry also boasts a comprehensive blog and resource section brimming with valuable information. Their articles and tutorials cover a broad spectrum of podcasting topics, from technical aspects of audio production to strategies for building a loyal audience. The focus on practical, actionable advice makes Blubrry a valuable asset for both novice and experienced podcasters. Their frequently updated content ensures that you're always up-to-date with the latest industry trends and techniques.

For those seeking a more visual learning experience, **YouTube** is an invaluable resource. Search for channels dedicated to podcasting; you'll find countless tutorials and guides covering every aspect of the process. Look for channels focusing on specific software, equipment, or podcasting strategies. Many experienced podcasters create in-depth walkthroughs of their workflows, providing valuable insight into their techniques and best practices. The sheer volume of content on YouTube offers incredible flexibility in tailoring your learning experience to your specific needs and areas of interest. Remember to filter results by upload date to prioritize the most recent and relevant information.

Beyond individual websites, dedicated podcasting platforms offer community features and support forums. **Libsyn** , mentioned earlier as a podcast hosting provider, also has a robust community forum where podcasters can connect, ask questions, and share their experiences. This is an excellent opportunity to learn from others, troubleshoot technical issues, and benefit from collective wisdom.

The forum's active user base often provides quick solutions to common problems, making it a valuable support system for any podcaster facing challenges. Similarly, **Buzzsprout** fosters a vibrant community through its blog and occasional webinars. While not as extensive as some dedicated forums, their resources offer valuable insights into best practices and emerging trends. Engaging with their blog and attending their webinars can provide a valuable learning experience and networking opportunities.

Moving beyond specific platforms, let's explore broader online communities. **Reddit** has numerous subreddits dedicated to podcasting, offering a diverse range of discussions, advice, and support. Subreddits such as r/podcasting and r/podcasters provide a platform for sharing experiences, asking questions, and engaging with a vast community of podcasting enthusiasts. Remember to carefully review the rules and guidelines of each subreddit before participating in discussions. The sheer scale and diversity of opinions within these communities can be both overwhelming and incredibly beneficial.

Facebook groups dedicated to podcasting offer another avenue for connection and collaboration. Search for groups tailored to your specific podcasting niche or genre. These groups provide a space to connect with like-minded individuals, share your work, and get feedback. Remember to be mindful of group rules and etiquette, actively contributing to discussions rather than simply seeking self-promotion. The networking opportunities within these groups can lead to valuable collaborations and mutual support within your podcasting journey.

LinkedIn also proves surprisingly useful for podcasting professionals. While it might not seem the most obvious platform, many podcasting-related groups and professional organizations host discussions and share insights. Searching for relevant groups on LinkedIn can offer exposure to more experienced professionals and industry experts. Joining relevant groups can unlock opportunities for networking, collaboration, and discovering potential guests for your podcast.

Beyond these specific platforms, engaging in broader online discussions related to audio engineering, marketing, and content creation will greatly expand your knowledge and skills. Websites and forums related to these fields often contain information relevant to podcasting. For example, communities dedicated to audio editing software like Audacity or Adobe Audition frequently discuss techniques applicable to podcast production. Similarly, online resources for digital marketing and social media management offer valuable insights into audience building and podcast promotion. Don't limit your learning to podcasting-specific resources; broaden your horizons to unlock a wider range of knowledge and skills.

Finally, remember the importance of ongoing learning and adaptation. The podcasting landscape is constantly shifting, with new technologies, platforms, and strategies emerging regularly. Subscribe to newsletters, follow industry blogs, and actively engage with the online communities mentioned above to stay updated on the latest trends and best practices. Continuous learning will ensure that you remain competitive, adapt to changes, and constantly enhance the quality and reach of your podcast.

This list of websites and online communities serves as a starting point for your continued learning and engagement within the vibrant world of podcasting. Remember that active participation, consistent learning, and a willingness to collaborate are keys to sustainable success in this dynamic field. Utilize these resources to expand your knowledge, connect with fellow podcasters, and elevate your podcasting skills to new heights. The journey of podcasting is as much about the community and the continuous learning process as it is about the creation itself. Embrace this aspect of the journey, and you will undoubtedly benefit greatly. Consider using a dedicated notebook or digital document to keep track of the resources you find most useful, creating your own customized and personalized guide to the world of podcasting.

25

LEGAL CONSIDERATIONS FOR PODCASTERS

Navigating the legal landscape of podcasting can feel daunting, but understanding the fundamentals of copyright, licensing, and fair use is crucial for protecting yourself and your work. Ignoring these legal considerations can lead to costly lawsuits and damage your reputation. This section aims to demystify these concepts and provide you with the knowledge to create and distribute your podcast ethically and legally.

First, let's tackle copyright. Copyright law protects original works of authorship, including musical compositions, sound recordings, and literary works. Simply put, if someone creates something original, they automatically own the copyright to it. This means that using someone else's copyrighted material without permission is infringement, regardless of whether you're making money from it.

The penalties for copyright infringement can be severe, ranging from hefty fines to legal action. Therefore, always obtain the necessary permissions before using any copyrighted material in your podcast.

This includes music, which is a frequent source of copyright infringement issues for podcasters. Many podcasters mistakenly believe that using royalty-free music is a blanket solution. While royalty-free music allows for use without paying royalties per use, it still usually comes with a license that needs to be followed carefully. This license might restrict how you can use the music, where you can distribute your podcast, and even how you can modify the music itself. Always read the license agreement carefully before incorporating any royalty-free music into your podcast. Some royalty-free music providers, like PremiumBeat or Epidemic Sound, offer extensive libraries of music specifically licensed for use in podcasts and videos. These services provide clarity and peace of mind, although they do involve a subscription fee. It is often a worthwhile expense considering the potential legal ramifications of using unlicensed music.

Furthermore, even seemingly innocuous sound effects can be subject to copyright. Many websites offer free sound effects. Be sure to carefully verify their licensing terms. Creative Commons licenses, for example, offer various levels of permission, ranging from free use with attribution to non-commercial use only. Again, carefully review the license terms before incorporating any sound effects into your podcast. Failing to do so may inadvertently lead to copyright infringement. If you're unsure about the license, it's always best to err on the side of caution and seek out alternatives that are clearly and explicitly licensed for the intended use. It's better to spend time searching for legally-clear assets than to risk legal trouble.

Then we have the issue of using interviews in your podcast. While you own the copyright to the recording of the interview itself, you may not have the right to use the content your guest shares, i.e., reading selections from their book or quoting song lyrics. It's best to secure written permission from your guests before using their interviews in your podcast, especially if they share any copyrighted material, disclose confidential information, or discuss any trade secrets. Having a clear release form signed by your guests will protect you from any potential legal issues arising from their contributions. These forms should explicitly detail how their contribution will be used and distributed and ensure they understand the potential reach of your podcast. This careful approach establishes a professional relationship with your guests and safeguards your podcast from unnecessary risk.

Licensing offers a legitimate way to use copyrighted material. There are various types of licenses, each with its own terms and conditions. A comprehensive understanding of these licenses is necessary to ensure you use copyrighted material legally. Music licensing services, for instance, offer various licenses for different types of use, depending on your needs. These range from basic performance licenses to synchronization licenses, which allow you to use the music alongside visual elements. Choosing the appropriate license ensures you remain compliant and avoids legal pitfalls. Always thoroughly understand the specific terms of any license you acquire.

Fair use is an important legal principle that allows the limited use of copyrighted material without permission under certain circumstances. These circumstances generally involve transformative use, where the copyrighted material is used in a way that adds new meaning or message. However, fair use is a complex legal doctrine with no simple definition. The courts often evaluate the use based on several factors, including the purpose and character of the use, the nature of the copyrighted work, the amount and substantiality of the portion used, and the effect of the use on the potential market for the original work. Therefore, it's important to consult with a legal professional if you intend to rely on fair use as a defense in case of infringement.

To make your podcast a safe and legally sound project, consider including a disclaimer in your show notes disclosing any music or sound effects used and giving attribution to the copyright holders. This is especially relevant for content under Creative Commons licenses that require attribution. Transparency helps prevent misunderstandings and strengthens your position if any legal issues arise. Additionally, be sure to keep detailed records of all your sources for sound effects and music, including the license agreements, in case they are needed for future reference.

While using readily available online resources is convenient, you should prioritize accuracy and verification when sourcing information. Ensure your facts are correct and that you avoid making statements that are false or misleading. Similarly, be sure to properly cite any sources used in your podcast, to ensure that you aren't infringing upon intellectual property.

Beyond copyright and licensing, you should also be aware of other legal considerations, such as defamation and privacy. Defamation is making false statements about someone that harm their reputation.

Be cautious about making accusations or claims without solid evidence. Similarly, protect the privacy of your guests and others featured in your podcast. Avoid disclosing private information without their explicit consent.

The Take-Away

Consider consulting with a legal professional specializing in intellectual property law to get advice tailored to your specific situation. They can provide personalized guidance on navigating copyright issues and ensuring that your podcast complies with all relevant regulations. This proactive approach provides you with peace of mind, knowing you are making the right legal decisions while building your podcast. A lawyer's consultation, while potentially a financial investment, can be invaluable in preventing costly legal battles down the road. Remember, protecting your podcast and your reputation is paramount, and seeking expert legal advice is a wise investment. It's far more cost-effective to invest in legal counsel beforehand than to face the consequences of legal action later.

26
FINAL THOUGHTS

Building a sustainable podcast is a multifaceted endeavor that requires careful planning, consistent effort, and a resilient mindset.

By setting realistic goals, maintaining audience engagement, creating a sustainable workflow, fostering resilience, and adapting to the dynamic world of podcasting, you can create a podcast that not only thrives but also continues to grow and evolve over time. The journey may have its ups and downs, but with a well-defined strategy and unwavering commitment, your podcast can become a rewarding and fulfilling endeavor.

Remember, it's a marathon, not a sprint, and the rewards of consistent effort are immeasurable.

If it is a true passion, go for it! I've been podcasting on-and off in several different genres for twenty years, beginning with telephone conferences bridges and cassette recorders. Today I use many of the tools mentioned in this book in tandem to create a broadcast quality show that can easily be purposed across many platforms. I still get excited when I see an interview date pop up on my calendar and look forward to new ideas and new friendships which great conversations can foster.

Good luck with your adventures in podcasting. And write to me at Terry@TerryShepherd.com if you have questions or feedback.

ACKNOWLEDGMENTS

This is a book with many authors. My gratitude to the legions of broadcasters and podcasters who taught me what I know, to the excellent representatives of the products and platforms who were generous with their input and to my attorney friends who specialize in intellectual property law. This is a list too long to reproduce in a book this size. I am indebted to all who came before me for the creation of what you read today.

It's important to remember that our world is constantly changing. New technology supplants old. Social networks are born, grow, wither and die, replaced by the new shiny thing. Use whatever information you glean from this book as a guide to your own research on the topic, to ensure you are taking advantage of the latest updates and fresh thinking.

Non-fiction has become an unfamiliar space for a storyteller who specializes in the imagination. Special gratitude to Kerry Schafer for her editing skill in transforming my mechanical prose into something hopefully understandable and meaningful.

Finally, thanks to all of you who have read this far. We all have a story to share. Podcasts have empowered anybody and everybody to share them. Should you decide to join the community, we welcome you with open arms and wish you well!

ABOUT THE AUTHOR

Author Biography

Terry Shepherd is an author, podcaster, audio engineer, and broadcaster with a background in media production and online content creation. Terry has been podcasting since 2005 and interviewing interesting people on radio and television since 1970. He is the author of the *Jessica Ramirez Thrillers*, the covid classic *Juliette and the Mystery Bug* and *Curious Books* - a compendium of his short fiction. He currently hosts an author centric podcast, In Conversation With Terry Shepherd. Find out more about his adventures at Terry Shepherd.com.

Made in the USA
Monee, IL
08 November 2026

68012210R00090